THE LAST
DAYS OF
MAXIMILIAN
KOLBE

THE LAST DAYS OF MAXIMILIAN KOLBE

SERGIUS C. LORIT

new city press, new york

Forth Printing 1988

Published in the United States of America by New City Press,
the Publishing House of the Focolare Movement, Inc.
206 Skillman Avenue. Brooklyn, N.Y. 11211
© 1968 and 1981 by New City Press, Brooklyn, N.Y.
Revised edition translated from the original Italian edition
Kolbe, Cronaca degli Ultimi Giorni by New City Press
Printed in the United States of America
ISBN 0-911782-35-4
Library of Congress Catalog Card Number 80-82418

Nihil Obstat: Martin S. Rushford
           Diocesan Censor
Imprimatur: Francis J. Mugavero, D.D.
           Bishop of Brooklyn
           Brooklyn, N.Y. September 8, 1980

Contents

1

The Starvation Bunker

The snarl of a police dog drifted back from
the distant swamps, out there beyond the electrically charged fence. That meant they were still
looking for the escaped prisoner. And night was
fast coming on.

For the past three hours—three seemingly
endless hours—the prisoners in the concentration
camp had stood at attention, absolutely immobile,
with the machine guns of the SS trained upon
them. Lined up in huge companies along the four
sides of the great quadrangle, the prisoners hardly
seemed like human beings at all, but more like
grotesque mannequins. Thousands of identical
coats in neat vertical lines, draped over living
skeletons standing in a gigantic chamber of
horrors. The guards in the watchtowers ran the
muzzles of their machine guns up and down the
rows, zeroing in on each gaunt figure, one by one.

Up and down, up and down in the center of the

7

quadrangle walked "Bullneck" as they referred to the *Lagerführer,* Herr Fritsch. From beneath the visor of his cap, neatly blocked to a gothic arch, steel-gray eyes glared out. With his hands behind his back and his head, neck, and back forming one constant, rigid line, he marched ten steps forward, about-face, ten steps to the rear, about-face, again and again, his heavy boots pounding the dirt with metronomic regularity. In the frightening silence of the evening, the echo of those footsteps could be heard bouncing back from some of the camp's long, low buildings.

Three hours before, at 6 p.m. of a day in late July or early August, 1941 (in the accounts of the surviving witnesses the placing of the exact date differs, varying along the length of a one week period), the platoons (or "blocks") of prisoners had returned in their usual way from a day of forced labor. At that time of year, the usual pick-and-shovel work was interrupted for a few days in order to harvest the wheat and barley from the little patches of ground not yet claimed by the marshes.

Lined up inside the bleak quadrangle, they all had answered the evening roll call—that is, all except one. One prisoner's number, repeated again and again, brought no response; the man was from Block 14.

The alarm system sounded, dogs and guards went out to hunt down the escaped inmate, while back on the quadrangle the first flurry of official excitement gave way to a siege of mass retaliation.

For one hundred eighty eternal, terror-filled

minutes they stood there, the cramps brought on by their forced position of immobility seeming nothing compared to the dread that filled their souls. "My God, what will happen to us now?" each prisoner in Block 14 asked himself. "Who will have to pay for this? Will it be me?...What is going through old Bullneck's maddened brain? Oh, if he'd only stand still awhile! Back and forth, back and forth, like a clock pendulum ticking off someone's doom! Will it be mine? Stop it, you devil!...I'll gladly settle for the firing squad. One shot, and it would be all over.... Or even hanging on the gallows wouldn't be so bad. But not the Bunker! Anything but the Bunker!"

The concentration camp was situated in southern Poland, where the Sola flows into the Vistula. It was built on the ruins of several farm houses and barracks which had been razed by Hitler's *blitzkrieg.* The air was unhealthy, and the surrounding region, much of it marshes, was deserted. For Hitler's forces had deported the entire population elsewhere, so that no loose-tongued witness could disturb the secrecy with which their factory of death was to carry out its work. Unknown to the vast majority of German citizens, the "new order" was to have its beginnings in just this kind of secret "laboratory."

The Polish call this region Oswiecim, and so this gloomy complex of brick buildings enclosed with barbed wire was called Camp Oswiecim. The Nazis called it Camp Auschwitz. Auschwitz could accommodate 200,000 prisoners, and the smoke of its crematories went up night and day. A special commission had even been appointed to give the whole process of extermination a scientific basis of organization and procedure, and was committed to a plan for progressively increasing the output of the funeral ovens, year by year. It was Himmler's purpose (and we have written documentation of this) to make Auschwitz the cornerstone of a vast *Himmlerstadt* (city of Himmler) which after the final triumph of Hitler's forces was to house ten million enslaved people at the service of Greater Germany. It was to be a gigantic production plant operating at rock-bottom cost, and also an immense "refuse receptacle" where the offscourings of the racial selection process could be at the same time exploited and eliminated. Once carried out to its logical consequences, this process of selection was to have brought about—first in Europe, but later in the entire world—a perfected race of human beings.

And, in fact, by the end of the war Auschwitz could be viewed as a complete incarnation of Himmler's ambition—on the experimental level, at least. At that time evidence indicated that better than five million human beings had been reduced to ashes in its crematories.

The same thing had happened, in varying degrees, at Belsen, Mauthausen, Dachau, Buchenwald, and other Nazi concentration camps. But Auschwitz had been honored as the first to install gas chambers (or "shower and disinfection rooms" as the signs over the entrances called them) and it was unique in another way also. It had something absolutely original to its credit, a barbaric invention that was the pride and joy of Lagerführer Fritsch: the Starvation Bunker.

At 9 p.m. sharp, Herr Fritsch ceased his endless pacing in the middle of the quadrangle. He barked an order, and it was relayed to every block: "Break ranks!"

They brought soup from the kitchens, and a kettle of it was also taken over to the men in Block 14, but no one was allowed to have any. They kept it there, allowing it to give off its fragrance before all those hunger-crazed eyes, until the dripping of saliva from the prisoners' mouths told them they had achieved the effect they desired. Then slowly, savoring the torture they were inflicting, they took it to the edge of the field and emptied it down a drain.

The prisoners of Block 14 were sent to their bunks that night, but no one got any sleep. For while hunger gnawed away at their stomachs, a maddening fear clawed away inside their minds. They were terrified by thoughts of the Bunker.

No sense pretending. Everyone knew that after the last two prison breaks had been discovered, Fritsch had proceeded each time, personally, to choose ten special victims from the escapee's own block. And the story was always the same: the door of the Bunker had closed behind those victims, and none of them returned.

The Bunker was dug out below Block 13. The barracks above it differed in no way from the rest, except for the block number, which was painted in black. The ground floor provided quarters for "Discipline Company," which looked after the summary execution of anyone guilty of the slightest act of insubordination. All around Block 13 were gallows provided for this purpose.

But that night the prisoners in Block 14 were not afraid of the gallows, but of the underground chambers beneath them. Down there, the cells were completely bare: no windows, no bunks to lie on—nothing but a dirty bucket in the corner that served as a toilet. Two of these cells were being used at the time of our story—occupied by twenty men condemned to a slow, agonizing death.

When Bullneck's perverse mind dreamed up the Bunker, he hit upon the very quintessence of refined cruelty as a method of execution. It was a slow agony, drawn out for days and days. The victim felt his intestines drying up, his veins burning with fire, his brain exploding again and again with madness. Death descended, drop by drop, yet each droplet was loaded with intensity. Men, in the process, lost all vestiges of their humanity, so that in their death agonies even wolves would not be safe in their presence. Death by starvation, yet the deprivation went beyond mere hunger. As Herr Kommandant Fritsch saw it, mere starvation was not severe enough a punishment. Thirst was what gave the final touch, and this was the magic ingredient added to complete his sadistic invention.

Block 13 was enclosed by a twenty-foot wall,

and no one dared go near it, on pain of instant death by hanging. Those who must pass through that wall and descend into the Bunker could consider themselves "buried alive" from that moment on. All communication with the outside world was finished, and no one on the outside could give them any message. Once a day the SS men of "Discipline Company" descended into the Bunker, opened the cell door, and had Bruno Borgowiec—a Polish prisoner who served as interpreter, secretary, and undertaker for Block 13—remove the bodies of those who had died during the last twenty-four hours, after which they would be taken to the cremation ovens. If anyone begged them for a piece of bread or a mouthful of water, the SS men would respond with curses and kicks in the stomach. "That's how it will be till the last condemned man is dead," they told each other that night in Block 14. And with good reason, for as long as Auschwitz continued to operate, no one ever came out of the Starvation Bunker alive.

Next day, the prisoners from all the blocks were assembled in the quadrangle. At roll call, Fritsch announced that the escapee had not been found. Then everyone was marched away—except those in Block 14.

So then, while the other blocks, each with its escort of armed roughnecks, went to finish the harvest out among the fetid marshes, the men of Block 14 were prepared to face a special retribution, which would be much more intense than the previous evening's collective punishment.

Surrounded by the steel-helmeted SS with leveled machine guns, these men who already suffered from months of scanty provisions and who had eaten nothing at all for twenty-four hours, were again stood at attention, immobile beneath the hot summer sun that beat down more pitilessly with every passing hour. No one was allowed even a drop of water.

Every half hour one of the guards would walk between the ranks, arbitrarily striking this or that prisoner with a savage blow from his rifle butt. The muzzles of firearms were trained on them from every angle, ready to spit hot lead at anyone who showed the least sign of resistance.

The hours seemed like centuries, as the sun burned into their shaved heads; their throats became more and more parched with thirst, and their muscles became contorted with terrible cramps. At last some of them began to drop to the ground, exhausted. If they did not come to life again under the blows of SS boots, then they were dragged away by their feet to one corner of the quadrangle. And as the hours passed, a large pile of them were heaped, one on top of another, in the great assembly area. Those who held out amid all this treatment felt their faces becoming terribly swollen and saw spots dancing in front of their eyes.

Finally, at 3 p.m., there was time out for half an hour of late-afternoon lunch. Even this concession was part of Bullneck's cool calculations—a means of ensuring that everyone did not collapse before evening, when the martyrdom of martyr-

14

doms would begin for the ten men he personally intended to select for this purpose. As soon as the meal was over, the poor wretches were again lined up, and remained standing at attention until sunset.

At six o'clock the other blocks returned to camp, passing, as they did every day, beneath the arch at the camp entrance, which mockingly greeted them with its cynical inscription: *Arbeit macht frei!* ("Work brings freedom!") There was the usual formation for roll call in the quadrangle.

Lagerführer Fritsch heard the reports of his lieutenants, then proceeded to where the prisoners of Block 14 were standing. Two paces behind him came the *Raportführer,* Palitsch, his adjutant, and at a distance of a few yards a semicircular cluster of SS men, heavily armed.

The Kommandant stood before his victims with feet planted far apart, and deathly silence fell upon the camp. Fritsch allowed himself a few minutes to enjoy the uncomfortable stillness, before breaking it with his announcement: "The fugitive has not been recovered. Therefore ten of you must die in the Starvation Bunker. Next time, it will be twenty."

The sentence of judgment had been given, and every member of Block 14 felt its effects. Cold sweat collected on each sun-scorched brow. "It's my turn this time. . . . Execution, at last, my execution! Oh, Lord, let me die, but not this way, please. . . ."

Bullneck walked past the first row and made his choice, then another, then a third. He carefully scrutinized each prisoner, savoring the look of

15

terror he saw on each face. The slow rhythm of his footsteps gave the effect of a funeral march. Fritsch loved to appear dramatic, and no doubt his ears heard the pounding strains of Wagnerian music as he passed among those living shades like the angel of death.

He would stop very suddenly in front of each condemned man, commanding him in bad Polish: "Open your mouth! Show me your teeth! Stick out your tongue!" Then he would linger in front of each victim for a minute inspection of his oral cavity, with the air of a meat inspector at the slaughter house. On what basis did he make his selections, everyone wondered. Was it the strongest or the weakest he chose to liquidate? Who could tell? Actually the selections were more or less arbitrary and the "health inspection" was just a detail added for dramatic effect.

After each oral examination Fritsch would point to the prisoner's number, sewed to the left side of his shirt. "This one!" he would say, and Palitsch would add the number to his list of condemned men.

One by one the selected victims were removed from the ranks, pale and crestfallen, until the death roster was complete. "So long, friends," one of them told his comrades remaining in line. "We'll meet again up there, when real justice is meted out!"

"Long live Poland!" a young man cried out. "If it is for her that I give my life."

Then there was the hopeless, uncontrollable

16

sobbing of a father: "My poor wife, my poor children. Goodbye, goodbye!" (This was Sergeant Francis Gajowniczek who thus wailed and wept, head in hands.)

"Take off your shoes!" said the SS, and ten pairs of wooden clogs lay empty on the ground. This too was part of the prescribed ritual: sending the victims barefoot to their place of execution. Meanwhile, among the remaining ranks of Block 14 prisoners, terror had given way to a sense of soothing relief. After so many hours of anxious tension, many a heart leaped momentarily for joy.

One who has never personally lived through an experience as the inmate of a concentration camp could find it very difficult to understand, let alone justify, certain attitudes that develop there. The gnawings of hunger that grow on you day by day could drive you to attack a fellow prisoner, as emaciated as yourself, just to get his piece of bread. Those bloodhounds prey upon you with inhuman ferocity, and for no logical reason that you know of. Hour by hour they debase your personality methodically, according to a carefully arranged scientific procedure. Before they kill you, they want to tear you to pieces, destroy you.

To have "survived" meant more than a mere holding onto life for those not among the select few of Block 14. It meant escape from the most cruel of all deaths. Yet it was here, among these who had escaped death by hunger, while everyone was sighing with relief, that one man was making an unprecedented decision.

17

This man, bearing the number 16670, stepped boldly out of line and walked with a decisive step toward Herr Kommandant. Whispers passed like a gust of wind from one block to another all across the great quadrangle: "Who's that?" "What's he doing?" "What could he be up to?" "Is he plumb crazy?"

None of the old-timers of Auschwitz could ever remember anyone daring to break ranks without a specific command to do so, and this man had actually come out in the open and was approaching old Bullneck himself.

Such an infraction of the camp's iron discipline was so utterly fantastic and incredible that it gave rise to two other incredible and fantastic happenings. First of all, the many guards in attendance, accustomed to pulling the trigger whenever a suspicious movement of any kind occurred, did not now fire a shot. And then the awestruck Lagerführer, seeing the prisoner approach with such a firm step, reached down and whipped a .38 out of his boot. "Halt!" he gasped. "What does this Polish pig want with me?"

Then another wave of subdued whispers went through the lines: "It's Father Kolbe!"

"It is! It's Father Maximilian Kolbe himself."

"The Franciscan from Niepokalanów!"

So number 16670 became a name once more. He was Father Maximilian Kolbe, founder of Niepokalanów, the City of the Immaculate. But what did this "Polish pig" want with a full-blooded German like Fritsch?

Removing his hat, he stood at respectful attention in front of the camp commander. His kindly eyes were as calm and smiling as his parched features would allow them to be. His face was pale to the point of transparency, and his head was inclined slightly to the left side.

Almost in a whisper he said in German: "I would like to die in the place of one of these men," motioning with his hand to the little group of ten condemned to the Bunker, separated from one another by SS men.

A shadow of amazement flitted over the angry features of Herr Fritsch. What he had just heard was so far beyond his powers of comprehension, that for a moment he began to wonder if he was dreaming.

But he wasn't dreaming. The omnipotent ruler who allowed no exception to his commands, the unbending autocrat who never reversed a decision, the butcher of men who could stop any rebel in his tracks with a bullet from his .38, when he met this man's look of serenity could find only one word to answer him: "*Warum* (Why)?"

Never before had Lagerführer Fritsch addressed any "man with a number" in his camp, much less carried on a conversation with him.

Father Kolbe knew that any semblance at this point of playing the "hero" could lose him all he hoped to gain. He had better help the executioner save face, because at the moment he was obviously on the spot. Thus at this point he invoked an unwritten but basic statute of Nazi law in order to

19

plead his case: *The sick and the weak must be liquidated.* "I am an old man, sir, and good for nothing. My life is no longer of use to anyone...."

"...And in whose place do you want to die?" Fritsch broke in with a gasp, getting more excited every minute.

"For him, the one who has a wife and children," and with his hand he pointed beyond the steel helmets of the SS to Sergeant Francis Gajowniczek, still sobbing, head in hands.

"And just who are you?" snapped Fritsch.

"A Catholic priest."

He didn't say "a religious" or "a Franciscan" or "founder of the Militia of Mary Immaculate." He just said "a priest." It was just enough information to give Fritsch a good pretext for reversing his decision.

Priests occupied the second lowest "rung" of the camp ladder, as far as the Auschwitz SS were concerned. (Perhaps "concerned" is an inappropriate word to attribute to these rulers of the barbed wire jungle!) The lowest rung was reserved for members of the Jewish race. But immediately after the Jewish swine came *die schweinerischen Pfaffen* ("priest pigs"). These were assigned the most strenuous work, and upon them blows of the lash most often descended. Humiliated, almost beaten to death, reduced to mere human wrecks, they were constantly hunted down by the hate mongers as though they were mad dogs.

"*Ein Pfaffe!*" sneered the Lagerführer, with a meaningful look at Palitsch. In that lurid sneer Father Kolbe could detect with certainty that his

20

request had been approved. "Accepted," was in fact the reply that Fritsch gave him. Palitsch drew a line through number 5659, belonging to Sergeant Gajownizeck, and in its place on the list wrote Father Kolbe's number: 16670.

Everything was in order, the roster of victims complete, yet the whole camp was in a state of stupefaction. Never before in the history of Auschwitz had it happened that a prisoner had offered his own life in place of someone else completely unknown to him.

In that dismal kingdom of hatred, the dazzling brilliance of this act of love had overcome the darkness.

The victims were ordered to undress, retaining only a tattered undershirt. Then, in this almost naked state, and barefoot, they were marched single file to the Bunker. Last in the pathetic line-up was Father Kolbe, his head still inclined a little to the left, his lips murmuring a prayer: "My Queen, my Lady, my Mother...*Mamusia*...you have kept your word. For this hour I was born!" And his heart sang of heaven.

Beyond the electrically charged wires of the stockade, the setting sun touched the horizon, and then the great flaming disk plunged into the distant marshes and out of sight. The sky was painted the color of martyrs.

The few surviving witnesses of that Auschwitz sunset in late July, 1941 would later declare: "It was a magnificent sunset, such as we had never seen."

By the time the ten men had passed through

the forbidden wall, the shades of night had begun to descend over the camp. There was darkness in the Bunker also. Thick as the cell walls had been built, they could not muffle completely the inhuman wailing emitted by those twenty already buried alive, as they voiced the torment of their collective agony. They had been there several days already, condemned to die of thirst and starvation by the irreversible decree of Herr Fritsch.

"Undress!" said the SS of "Discipline Company." Overcome with fear, the ten obeyed in haste, removing their one remaining garment. In that moment Father Kolbe thought of Jesus dying naked on the cross, and he also obeyed—out of love. Then a door was opened, and the ten of them were unceremoniously shoved inside the dark cell.

When the door closed upon them, not only every ray of light but every glimmer of hope for survival was finally spent. From that moment on, nothing—absolutely nothing—would be given them to keep the flame of life burning. This was the moment when for each and all began the longest and cruelest of agonies—the last, seemingly eternal, tragic chapter in each one's life history. And the testimony of those moments would remain sealed forever in the secrecy of a horrid grave.

Or so it might have been, had not one witness survived to describe that last chapter. This man was Bruno Borgowiec, Polish secretary, interpreter, and official undertaker for the Bunker. Only by means of his descriptions can we reconstruct those last days with any exactness.

The SS left, one after another, and the last, as he closed up the Bunker, hurled back these terrifying words: *"Ihr werdet eingehen wie die Tulpen!"* ("You will all wither away like tulips!"), punctuating the aptness of his metaphor with an emphatic slam of the door.

They say that at that very moment, on a street in Cracow, an elderly woman dressed in black collapsed on the sidewalk. The passersby who helped her to her feet heard her murmuring, "My son, my son...."

This woman was Maria Dabrowska, mother of Maximilian Kolbe. Once she had aspired to become a nun, but could not get permission. Now she was satisfied to live with the Felician Sisters and look after a few domestic affairs.

That day she had gone to run a couple of errands for her community, when, with a sudden telepathic insight, she saw her son shut up in an underground chamber, and she knew at once that he had been condemned to death by starvation. The thought of it had caused her to faint.

But in that vision she saw her son smiling at her, singing with confidence to the Virgin Mary and exhorting her to join him in hymns to Mary Immaculate.

2

The Kolbe Household

Auschwitz, first week of August, 1941. In the darkness of the Starvation Bunker, the slow death decreed by Lagerführer Fritsch was minute by minute, hour by hour, day by day, relentlessly consuming the ten innocent victims of Block 14.

Most of them, that is. Some had died quickly, and Borgowiec had hauled them away to the crematorium. "But it doesn't even seem like the dreaded Starvation Bunker," Borgowiec muttered to himself. "When I go down there, it's like descending into the crypt of a church. It was never like this before."

Several years later, this same Bruno Borgowiec would narrate the details of that slow death undergone by Father Kolbe and his companions: "From the cell where these unfortunates were buried alive, every day you could hear the sound of religious hymns and of the rosary and other prayers being recited aloud. And the condemned men from other cells would join in. I had to go down at least once a day to accompany the guards on their tour of inspection. They would always have me take away the corpses of those who had succumbed to their sufferings during the night.

"Also, when the guards were not around, I would sometimes sneak in alone in order to speak a few words with my unfortunate countrymen and comfort them the best I could. Every time I went down there, the place would be filled with the sound of fervent prayers and hymns to the Blessed Virgin. Father Maximilian Kolbe would start them out; then everyone would join in.

"Sometimes they would be so absorbed in prayer that they would not even realize the guards had come for the daily inspection and had opened the door of their cell. Only when the SS began shouting at them would they stop praying."

The days of really urgent hunger came upon them, and yet Father Kolbe and his companions never gave way to the rabid despair that Fritsch had planned for them, in which every trace of a man's humanity would be burned out of him and the instincts of a tortured animal would take over completely.

"When the cells were opened," says Borgowiec, "the poor wretches would beg for mercy, crying out loudly for just a piece of bread and a little swallow of water. When one of the stronger ones managed to get near the door and reach out his arms in supplication, the guards would kick him in the stomach, and send him sprawling backward onto the cement floor. If this did not break his neck and bring instant death, then a bullet would be used to finish him off.

"To give you an idea what these prisoners went through," Borgowiec relates bluntly, "I need only mention that I never needed to empty the bucket in the corner. It was always empty and dry. The sufferers actually drank its contents in order to placate their thirst.

"In those days Father Kolbe displayed real heroism. He asked for nothing and never complained. He inspired the others with courage, urging them to hope that the fugitive from Block 14 would still be found, and that they would then be set free."

Father Maximilian Kolbe was born at Zdunska Wola, forty-seven years before the events recorded above. Zdunska Wola was a very poor town, part of a complex of similarly miserable small cities and towns whose economic center of gravity was the industrial city of Lodz. Lodz provided the inhabitants of these cities and towns with their only source of livelihood, and was at the same time the cause of their grinding, humiliating poverty.

Life as it was lived in Zdunska Wola (where everyone, male and female, was a weaver of cloth) was a very precarious, disagreeable sort of existence. Once a week the inhabitants went to the city, received their raw materials, and returned home. Back in their cottages they worked from dawn to the wee hours, day after day, always bent over their looms, in order to have as much finished cloth as possible to present to the merchants of Lodz, who paid them for their toil with a little handful of change.

Among the workers of Zdunska Wola—herself a worker's daughter, naturally—was Maria Dabrowska, a slender, ambitious young woman, who ever since she could remember had dreamed of becoming a nun, "in order to go to heaven and be with the pure souls there," as she told some of her confidantes.

Other girls her age were amusing themselves on Sundays by playfully parrying the first admiring glances of local young men, and tormenting themselves with thoughts so typical of this stage in life—"If he doesn't marry me, I'll die!" Maria Dabrowska also thought of death, and prayed for it, but her motivation was quite different. "I would rather die," she said, "than reach a marriageable age." And this, in her simplicity, was the prayer she regularly offered to God.

To understand her desire, one must realize that a Polish girl in her day, once she reached the proper age, had no choice but to marry. In this Russian-occupied section of the former kingdom of Poland, there was no written law to this effect, but the norms of ancient traditions and family customs were every bit as binding as law, if not more so.

In addition, there was the fact that the czarist occupiers had wanted to do away with convents having ties with Rome, and had decreed their closing (although some of the braver nuns continued on in their vocation secretly, dressed in civilian clothes). The few convents that had been able to remain open did not welcome the poorer class of girls, especially those like Maria who possessed nothing at all. The persons in whom Maria confided pointed this out to her.

Faced with this crude reality she kept praying to the Lord with the same basic formula, now intensely familiar to her. But since she was fundamentally a practical young woman, educated in the school of hard knocks, and thus accustomed to letting the cutting edge of her dreams be dulled by necessity, she began adding an epilogue to the original request: "Nevertheless, Lord, I don't want to tell you what to do. If your plans are otherwise, then at least give me a husband who doesn't swear or drink alcohol and who doesn't spend his time hanging around the taverns. This much, Lord, I'll have to insist on unconditionally." And as she got to this final request of her prayer, her voice would become fervently emphatic and insistent.

Of course, Maria Dabrowska realized she had to do her part in order to obtain an answer to her prayer. And so it happened that one evening when a fair-haired young man knocked at the door and with a timid smile asked for her hand in marriage, papa Dabrowski's consent came as no more than an echo of the choice she had made some time earlier.

Julius Kolbe was a very mild person in contrast to the energetic Maria. He was as close-mouthed as she was talkative, as gentle and submissive by nature as she was brash (at least occasionally). A year younger than his bride, he was a young man completely devoid of vices. Not only had he never tasted alcohol nor seen the inside of the Zdunska Wola tavern, but he was also averse to smoking.

As a worker he represented a classic breed that seems in danger of becoming extinct: for him, his work was more than something he had to do; it was a sacred duty. Any free time was dedicated to the Church, for he was a devout man and a member, indeed an officer, in the Third Order of St. Francis. Nothing could please Maria Dabrowska more than this, for she was not only as industrious and devout as her husband, but also belonged to the Third Order.

On October 5, 1891, Maria Dabrowska, aged twenty-one, was married to Julius Kolbe, aged twenty, and from the very first day of their marriage Mrs. Kolbe was the one who managed the family business.

Theirs was a one-room home, with the kitchen in one corner, the looms for weaving in another, while along one wall, behind a large flowered drapery, was the bedroom, equipped with two chests of drawers. Between these two pieces of furniture, beneath a painting of Our Lady of Czestochowa, they erected a kind of altar, adorned with a few other religious images and illuminated with oil lamps after the typical fashion of respectable Polish families. Amid these surroundings, in 1892, their first son Francis was born. And on January 8, 1894, their son Raymond, the future Father Maximilian, first saw the light of day.

Raymond, a lively, obstinate, often mischievous little fellow, was just learning to take his first steps, following the lead of big brother Francis, already an expert, when it became evident that the family would have to seek new quarters. The little room had thus far endured the give-and-take of married life and the incessant activities of the weavers' looms, but it soon proved inadequate for the antics of two boisterous youngsters such as these.

For this reason, and because the squalid poverty of Zdunska Wola offered the family a dim prospect for getting ahead, the Kolbes decided to move to Lodz. They remained there only a short time, however, before moving again to nearby Jutrzkowice, and finally to Pabianice. The city of Pabianice was also part of the miserable Lodz syndicate, but Pabianice possessed a slightly cleaner, more respectable kind of poverty that did not seem quite so dismal and discouraging to them.

Near a graveyard they were able to rent a little cottage for a modest amount of money, complete with the characteristic stork's nest on the roof. So here they brought their few sticks of furniture and their little altar, set up their looms, and engaged another weaver to use some of the space in their new workshop. To augment the family income, Maria Dabrowska opened a small secondhand shop, and Julius Kolbe rented three small plots of land and began raising vegetables. A few years of working almost night and day, and the Kolbe family found their economic condition had improved to the point of being bearable.

Meanwhile Joseph, the third son, had been born, and also Valentine and Anthony, but the latter two died in early childhood.

Between nursing and rearing her children, and running her store, Maria Dabrowska also managed to pick up the few notions necessary for her to become a midwife. Understandably, in her time and place the preparation for this profession consisted much more of practice than of theory.

As requests for assistance began to pour in for Maria Dabrowska, who could serve both as midwife and practical nurse, this came to be a steady occupation, providing her with a fairly dependable though modest income. Nothing to be sneezed at, anyway.

And as Raymond grew bigger he turned out to be very fast with figures, so that he could start helping in the store. This gave his mother more time to spend with her patients.

This improved financial condition fit into the family plans in more ways than one. When the Kolbes opened their store, settled their accounts, and took stock of future possibilities, they concluded that Providence was pointing in the direction of "school" for one of their boys. "To send a boy to school" in their way of talking was equivalent to "offering him to the Lord." Any other interpretation would never have entered their minds.

Francis, being the firstborn, was the logical candidate for such an honor. But the Kolbes decided that neither was Raymond going to experience the hardships they had gone through in their youth. He would become a businessman, and their own little business would now serve as the first stepping-stone for him in his upward march. As for Joseph, it was still too early to plan his future.

Raymond was no longer the headstrong, restless boy he had been at one time. Though not yet the meek and mild youth that friends would call "Marmalade," he was affectionate, lively, alert, and seldom disrespectful of others.

Maria Dabrowska's educational methods might be considered harsh by the devotees of present-day standards. After all, her hand was a trifle heavy, and her approach rather militaristic. But no one can deny that her severity produced some amazing results.

Raymond, being the most active of her boys, was usually the one to receive the severest punishments, but, as Maria Dabrowska has since told us, "he was also different in his attitude toward punishment. Whenever he had been up to some mischief, he would go to get the instrument of judgment himself. Then he would stretch himself out on the bench and, after receiving his just deserts, he would thank us and put the stick back where it belonged."

While his mother concerned herself with forming morally sound characters, his father played an equally energetic role in helping Raymond and his brothers to grow up with healthy bodies. "Whenever we had our first snowfall," one of Raymond's schoolmates tells us, "his dad would take them out to the garden for a barefoot race."

And together the parents saw to it that their children not only learned to read and write, but also received religious instruction. This was given them by Father Wladimir Jakowski, who taught them, besides catechism, a smattering of Latin.

It was sometime between the seventh and tenth years of his life that the most remarkable experience of Raymond's childhood occurred. This incident was one that he himself jealously kept a secret, never revealing it either to his childhood companions or to those of his later life. It came to light only after he had been dead a few years, when his secret was disclosed by the one person who ever knew about it: Maria Dabrowska.

As a neighbor later recalled: "Raymond was always bubbling over with life. He told me he felt as happy as St. Francis ever had, and that he wished that he could talk with the birds, as that saint had."

Perhaps it was a real "Franciscan" tendency in his soul, or perhaps it was just his typical childish admiration and envy for those of his friends who owned some pet that they could play with and look after. At any rate, he secretly bought a bird's egg, which he then tried to incubate in a neighbor's hen house. He was going to have his own bird, even if the poor creature was of rather humble pedigree, the kind that scratched for a living.

The neighbor informed Maria Dabrowska of his bird-raising enterprise, and she, with her high regard for the "perspiration value" of family funds, felt Raymond was carrying things too far. The whipping he got for it was uncommonly vigorous.

Yet the especially painful physical penalty he suffered for his crime was not what bothered him most. Rather, it was something his mother had said as she was carrying out the sentence, her voice sounding utterly heartbroken: "Tell me, my son, what is ever going to become of you?"

In the days that followed, Maria Dabrowska noticed a startling change in her son's behavior. For one thing, he made more visits than usual behind the curtain that concealed the family altar, and he would remain there for long periods of time, on his knees, weeping, before the image of Our Lady of Czestochowa. Or down at the village chapel he would spend a lot of time weeping before the altar of the Blessed Mother.

And every time he emerged from the Pabianice church or from behind the curtain at home, he would have such a beatiful expression on his face, and be so good, that Maria Dabrowska began to wonder if her child was ill. Finally she began questioning him about what had happened.

Raymond gave her no answer at first, just hung his head in silence. But the mother knew her child well enough to get over this hurdle. She knew the right chords to play on to awaken a response and overcome his shyness.

"Listen, Raymond," she told him, "you know you should tell your mother everything. You wouldn't want to be *disobedient*, would you?" Confronted with the issue of obedience to his mother, there was no secret in the world he would have kept back.

But we'll let Maria Dabrowska tell the story herself: "Trembling all over with emotion and with tears in his eyes, he told me: 'After that day you scolded me, mother, when you asked me what ever was going to become of me, I prayed often to Our Lady, asking her to show me what would happen. One day when I was in church and praying very hard, Our Lady appeared to me. She had two crowns in her hand. One was white and the other red. She looked at me lovingly and asked me which of the two crowns I wanted. The white one meant I would remain chaste; the red one was a martyr's crown. I told her I'd like them both. Then Our Lady smiled at me very sweetly and disappeared.'

"What convinced me that my boy was telling the truth was his radical transformation. From that day on, he was not the same as before, and often he would come to me with a radiant face to speak to me about his future martyrdom, as though this were his most cherished ambition. And I prepared myself for it, just as Our Lady did after she heard Simeon's prophecy."

Meanwhile Francis, the oldest boy, had begun to attend classes at the commercial high school. The Russians had closed up quite a few schools in their zone of occupation, and what few had stayed open were expensive to attend. Those living in the Pabianice area who wanted to continue their studies had little choice except the business school. The Kolbes resigned themselves to sending Francis there for the moment, trusting the Lord to provide for future needs.

For Raymond this was the beginning of his tour of duty, relieving his mother of her work in the store and at home. He was very efficient with housework. "He was always right there to help me, all the time," says Maria Dabrowska, "and was always surprising me at mealtime with some new recipe he had invented."

As a store clerk, however, he did not have such spectacular success. Not that he had any problem with mathematics—he had already demonstrated a remarkable aptitude for that subject, astounding everyone with his speed in all sorts of calculations and operations. No, figuring customers' accounts was definitely not a problem; but getting them to pay up was quite another story! One day papa Kolbe remarked, shaking his head, "My son, if you ever get to be a businessman, then I will be a bishop."

"And I will be a queen," said his mother.

One morning Maria Dabrowska needed to mix some medicine for a patient, and sent Raymond to the pharmacy for one of the necessary ingredients.

"Give me some *Vencon greca*," the boy told the druggist very nonchalantly, repeating the Latin words exactly as he had heard them from his mother.

"And what do you know about *Vencon greca*,"

the man asked in astonishment. In all his many years of practice in that town, the only time he had heard Latin spoken was by the priest at the altar.

"That's the Latin name of the stuff my mother wants," Raymond explained.

"And how did you know it was Latin, boy?"

"Oh, we get a few lessons from Father Jakowski."

"What do you mean, *we*? You and who else? What's your name? Where do you live? What school do you go to?"

Raymond told him that he and his brother Francis went to Father Jakowski for lessons, that they were sons of the Kolbes, who lived in the little cottage near the graveyard, that his brother was going to the business school, and that, God willing, he would eventually become a priest. He also told the man that he himself had to stay home and work because his parents didn't have enough money to send both of them to school.

"Young man," said the druggist, "it would be a crime to let this state of affairs continue. Would you consider coming to me for lessons? In a year's time I could have you caught up with your brother, and then you could both be ready for the second year, after final exams."

"That day," Maria Dabrowska would later recall, "Raymond came home floating on air, his eyes sparkling with joy as he told me of his good fortune. From then on, the pharmacist gave him lessons, and that wonderful, God-sent man taught

Raymond so well that he actually did catch up with his brother, and they were able to enter the sophomore class together."

Thus the attempt to make Raymond a businessman was very definitely set aside, even though, ironically, he and his brother had no other choice than to attend what was officially called a business school.

The next year passed quickly. During the Easter season of 1907 some Conventual Franciscans from a friary in Galicia came to Pabianice to preach a mission. The entire Kolbe family attended every preaching session "in formation." During the last service it was announced from the pulpit that a seminary high school had been opened at Lwów for the training of young men who felt a vocation to the Order of St. Francis. Raymond and Francis exchanged rapid and meaningful looks. Then afterwards, in the sacristy, they pleaded with the missionaries to let them enter the Order.

That very October the two boys said goodbye to their mother. Although Maria Dabrowska had looked forward eagerly to this moment, when it arrived she found it to be one of the most painful in her lifetime. Two of her sons were leaving for distant parts. Francis was only fourteen years old, and Raymond barely thirteen.

Papa Kolbe went with them most of the way, helping them to cross the border secretly into Austrian Poland and to board a train at Cracow. There he left them, lingering to wave his handker-chief at them until the last wisp of smoke from the engine was swallowed up in the distant clouds, in the direction of Lwów:

A few years later Julius Kolbe would also be seeing his third son Joseph off to a Franciscan school. Then the house would be empty, much too empty for him and his wife, and Mrs. Kolbe would again feel the call that had come to her as a girl, would speak openly to her husband about it, and would receive his encouragement to follow her belated vocation.

So it was that Maria Dabrowska set out to satisfy her lifelong desire for fuller consecration to God, and, at the same time, her need to be near her children. She soon found temporary lodging with the Benedictine sisters in Lwów, just a stone's throw from the Franciscan seminary. And when her sons were transferred to Cracow, she followed them there.

To have joined the Benedictines she would have had to renounce her membership in the Third Order of St. Francis, but at Cracow she experienced a real "homecoming" when she found a permanent residence with the Felician Sisters, who were themselves Third Order Franciscans.

Then papa Kolbe, left alone at Pabianice, decided to liquidate his weaving business and give up his land, so that he could also join the Franciscans as a Tertiary Oblate. But he found it difficult at his age to adjust to the religious life.

So Kolbe then went to Czestochowa, where every year the entire family had always gone on pilgrimage, even in hard times. There he lived alone, making his living from the sale of religious articles.

But soon he was moved by feelings of patriotism to join the movement for Poland's liberation from her czarist overlords. When World War I broke out in August 1914, he volunteered for the Russian front. When he was later taken prisoner, they discovered him in possession of a Russian passport—issued during the Russian occupation—tried him summarily as a traitor and hanged him at Olkusz. Poland will remember him as one of her many, many heroes in her struggle for national freedom.

Francis, Julius Kolbe's firstborn, also found it difficult, at the outbreak of the war, to resist the call of the liberation movement in its struggle to throw off the Russian yoke. He obtained a leave of absence from the Order and for three years served as an intelligence agent and a soldier, receiving a number of wounds in battle. At the end of the war he was declared in good health by the medics, but when he tried to return to his Order, he was declared "physically unfit for religous life."

Many years later, when Hitler started World War II by his attack on Poland, Francis Kolbe again joined up as an intelligence agent in the service of his nation.

In 1943 he fell into the hands of the Gestapo, and was shipped via cattle car to Auschwitz, arriving there two years after his brother, Father Maximilian Kolbe. What happened to Francis Kolbe after that has been lost to history.

3

Maximilian the Warrior

Auschwitz, second week of August, 1941. It seemed an eternity since that evening when the sun had set upon a deep red sky and the door of the Bunker had closed behind the ten prisoners from Block 14, who were to pay with the cruelest of tortures for the escape of one of their block mates.

Life was slowly ebbing out for those still holding on to it. Each day their voices, which had at first filled the whole underground prison with singing and prayer, were little by little losing their strength.

Bruno Borgowiec was always present for the daily SS inspections of the cell where Father Maximilian and his fellow sufferers lay dying. Concerning the beginning of this second week of starvation and terrible thirst, he was later to testify, as the only living witness: "Now that they were so terribly weakened in body, they had to recite their prayers in an undertone. At every inspection time, while almost everyone else was stretched out helplessly on the floor, Father Maximilian would greet us either standing or kneeling among the others with a look of serenity on his face. The guards, of course, knew that he had voluntarily offered his life for the sake of another prisoner who had a family to return to. They knew also that everyone here was being put to death unjustly. This seemed to give them a feeling of respect for Father Kolbe, and once I heard one of them remark to the others: *'Der Pfarrer dort ist doch ein ganz anständiger Mensch. So einen haben wir hier noch nicht gehabt.'* ('The priest is a real man. We never had one of his kind here before.')"

Thirty-four years earlier, in October 1907, a pleasant, thirteen-year-old Raymond Kolbe ("Marmalade" to his friends), accompanied by his brother Francis, left the commercial high school in Pabianice and entered the fledgling Franciscan seminary in Lwów to begin his study of the humanities.

Little is known about his three years of minor seminary, since the school's records did not survive the warfare and revolutions that later engulfed Lwów and its environs—today part of the Soviet Union. Our only evidence consists of a schoolmate's brief testimonial, a teacher's laconic remark, and a couple of curious facts. All emphasize a particular aspect of his personality.

Father Cornelius Czupryk once commented on Raymond as a fellow student, that he was "especially clever in the exact sciences and mathematics, so much so that the older fellows often turned to him when they had a hard problem to solve."

Mr. Gruchala, a layman who taught math at Lwów, is credited with observing on one occasion: "What a pity this young man is becoming a priest, with all the talents he has!"

As for the rest, we know that in his spare time Raymond drew up a set of plans for the strategic defense of Lwów. The plans were so extensive and so brilliant in their resolution of detailed problems, that they would have made a staff officer turn green with envy.

A second project the young seminarian worked on, also entirely in his spare time, was the design of spacecraft for interplanetary travel. Not only was he ahead of the science fiction craze by several decades, but in some respects his work was a remarkably accurate forecast of the space experiments of our own day.

In any case, after his three years of minor seminary, the group of priests who had to approve new admissions to the Order seem to have had no hesitation whatsoever in their acceptance of Raymond. So then, while he displayed brilliance and versatility in other fields, apparently he also impressed the good fathers that he was a lover of virtue and the Franciscan discipline, even though at the time he had done nothing remarkable to distinguish himself in the practice of religion.

But things did not go as smoothly as might have been expected. September 4, 1910, was the day set for him to receive his habit, but on the very eve of that ceremony he was suddenly beset by a crisis of conscience, or perhaps we should call it a vocational crisis.

Understandably, during those last few hours before his farewell to the world he experienced some anxiety, and his thoughts turned irresistibly backward to that day in the church at Pabianice, when the Virgin had offered him those two crowns, the white one and the red one. Time had not dimmed the memory of that splendid incident, but had etched it all the more vividly into his consciousness.

From then on, he remembered, all of his life, day by day, had been consecrated to the Blessed Mother, to *Mamusia,* as he now affectionately called her. The Polish language is especially rich in colloquial diminutives for *matka* (mother): *Mateczka, matuchna, matenka, mamulka,* etc. But *Mamusia* is the term used most frequently by very small children in addressing their mothers.

Raymond had no doubts about consecrating his future entirely to Mamusia, and as for the white crown he had accepted, he knew that personal purity was possible in just about any field of human endeavor. But what about the red crown of martyrdom?

Here was the source of Raymond's perplexity, where his mind wandered off into a maze of conjectures, for it had suddenly occurred to him that someone shut up in a cloister cannot easily become a martyr. That required getting out into the thick of battle. It would be a holy battle, of course, but still a very material conflict, in which he would fight in the defense of his Mamusia, his queen.

It seemed so clear to him now why God had given him such a talent for understanding the problems of science and technology. Surely this was the purpose of his innate love for the planning of strategy and for the study of military tactical maneuvers. It all appeared so clear in his mind, and the only thing that bothered him was that he had never thought of it before.

Thus he became convinced that at this eleventh hour he had found the direction his vocation should take. The first thing he did was to look up his brother Francis and demonstrate to him with great eloquence that a military career was the only thing for him, if by his life and his death he wanted to prove his loyalty to our Lady. His brother was so swayed by this presentation that he not only expressed his approval of Raymond's leaving the seminary, but said he was ready to accompany him.

There was not a minute to lose. They must see the provincial at once and let him know they would not be entering the novitiate, enumerating their reasons for the decision.

They were on the verge of entering the superior's cell when the doorbell rang and the porter opened the door of the visiting room. "Raymond! Francis!" It was Maria Dabrowska, who had spied her sons as soon as she entered the door. She ran to them with open arms. "I have wonderful news, boys, wonderful, happy news!"

Weeping with joy, she told them that their little brother Joseph, had decided to become a religious, "a Franciscan, just like you!" Their father Julius, she told them, had already gone to Cracow to enter a monastery—a Franciscan monastery—and she was going to enter the convent "here in Lwów with the Benedictines, but when they send you to Cracow, I can go to be with the Franciscans there!"

This unexpected visit at such a critical moment was for the two boys like a thunderbolt out of the blue. It immediately obliterated any "crisis" Raymond had felt about his vocation, and Francis, as one might expect, had no more problems either. And after their mother had kissed them both on the cheek, they felt there was something they had to do at once, and they did it. When they got in to see the provincial, they told him they were ready to become novices.

Nine years later Father Kolbe would write: "How can I ever forget that moment when Francis and I, awaiting. an appointment with Father Provincial to tell him we did not wish to enter the Order, heard the bell ring in the reception room. At that very delicate moment the God of providence, in his infinite mercy and through the services of Mary Immaculate, sent me my mother."

So, on the evening of September 4, 1910, before the altar of the Blessed Mother in the seminary chapel, Raymond Kolbe took the habit of St. Francis, and as he tied the cord around his waist he renounced his own given name and took instead that of Maximilian, which was very suggestive of the life he envisioned ahead of him.

A name inherited from the heroes of legend, it was the appellation of famous kings and emperors, and to the Austrians, who in those times occupied that section of Poland, it was a reminder of a glorious tradition. Under Maximilian I the Tyrol had been added to the Empire. The Turks had surrendered to Maximilian II in Belgrade. And everyone knew of "pure, dashing, handsome" Maximilian of Austria, who, after a short reign in Mexico, had been executed by a firing squad. And one of the heroes of the early Church had been Maximilian the martyr!

Raymond Kolbe's choice of a name fitted in well with his heroic ambitions. Barely sixteen years of age, he had an entire lifetime ahead of him to give to some glorious cause.

His novitiate lasted a year, during which time he was taught the Rule and Constitutions of the Order, and their significance in the life of a friar. As it happened, before many months passed by, the spirit of Francis of Assisi began to get through to Friar Maximilian, and the more he learned, the more he began to wonder if he could live up to it.

He was being afflicted, in other words, by a disease that is not uncommon among novices, and that is more painful than most people think it is. The malady is known officially as "scruples," and his superiors were well aware that there are no gentle remedies for it, nor pain relievers that one can take. The only effective cure requires a strong, drastic prescription: obedience. And this was the "medicine" they gave Friar Maximilian.

When he revealed his distress to his confessor, he was exhorted to commit himself without reservation to the spirit of the founder, and was reassured that all the obstacles could be overcome. After that, he was advised to open up to his novice master, who listened to him with great understanding. At the end, the novice master instructed him to henceforth confide every intimate thought, and even the slighest doubt that might arise, to his roommate, a novice who was older than himself and who had had more experience and more formation in the spiritual life.

Friar Maximilian obeyed at once, confiding everything to this roommate and following whatever advice he gave. Peace then seemed to return to his soul. But perhaps this therapy might not have been so effective, no matter how docilely he submitted to it, had he not also enjoyed the remarkable influence of a holy example.

This example came from a saintly young religious, Venance Katarzyniec, who was already suffering from serious illness and physical trials, but who was known for his lively intellect and great charity.

The simple witness of Friar Venance (who has since died, and is being considered for beatification) taught Friar Maximilian more than the young novice would ever have learned from reading books and listening to lectures. His simple, unassuming way of life showed by example how humility could be blended with an exceptional degree of brilliance, how the Rule could be rigorously observed even by one whose health was very delicate, and how physical sufferings could be borne with a radiant smile.

Seeing such saintliness in action helped Friar Maximilian rid his mind of any unrealistic impressions he might have had regarding the saints in general. From then on, the saints emerged from the pious caricatures to which most people had relegated them, and began to speak to him in convincing, straightforward language.

On September 5, 1911, Friar Maximilian Kolbe made his simple profession according to the Rule of St. Francis of Assisi, and according to the Constitutions of the Friars Minor Conventual. He was scarcely seventeen years old, yet already he felt a deep assurance that these temporary vows would one day become perpetual. The example of Venance Katarzyniec had decisively healed him of his hesitations. From now on, every sacrifice was to be transfigured into an act of love. Love, he had learned, would enable him to keep every promise.

As a professed friar, he was to study philosophy and theology, and so was transferred to Cracow. But he spent only a year in Cracow, leaving in October 1912 for Rome.

But again, not everything had gone smoothly. When the provincial had broken the news to him, a month ahead of time, that his superiors had decided to send him to Rome for philosophy at the Gregorian University and theology at the International Seraphic College, the young man's heart had sunk within him.

The problem was that Rome as a city suffered from a very low reputation in Poland, as it probably did in many other parts of Europe. All kinds of stories about the corruption and vice in the Eternal City made their rounds of the seminaries and religious communities. It was said that to get from their living quarters to the classroom, religious had to pass through infamous neighborhoods. And it seemed as though everyone returning from Rome would add a little more sensationalism to the tales already being circulated in the Polish novitiates and cloisters.

At eighteen Friar Maximilian Kolbe still had his white crown to defend. How far could he actually trust himself? He knew from his study of military science that a defeat is sometimes best avoided by refusing to do battle. He felt that the present circumstance was one such case. And besides, his health had not been very good for some time now, and who knew whether he could possibly finish his studies in a climate so different from what he was used to....

When he was given an opportunity to speak with the provincial, it was the latter line of argument he pushed the hardest, emphasizing repeatedly that because of his delicate health he really ought to remain in Poland. His superior, though rather unpleasantly surprised by all this, did finally cross out Friar Maximilian's name from the list of those departing. And the young friar drew a sigh of relief.

But by that evening he had second thoughts about his decision; he now saw it as an act of cowardice. A very noble sort of cowardice, no doubt! But the fact remained that he had not been prepared to do battle, and had therefore excused himself from it, all because he had lacked faith in God and in the help of his Mamusia.

After a sleepless night, he went early next morning to see his provincial. "Father," he confessed, "I regret that the thoughts I expressed to you yesterday afternoon represented my own personal desires in the matter. Now, I beg of you, do with me as you see fit, for I want above all else to be obedient."

The provincial looked at him wordlessly, then opened a drawer, took out a list, and wrote down Friar Maximilian Kolbe's name at the bottom of the column. Two months later the young man wrote his mother from Rome: "Things are not quite as bad here as I thought when I wrote you about them.... Besides, we never go anywhere except in groups."

Brother Maximilian completed his three years of philosophy at the Pontifical Gregorian University on October 22, 1915, and then began his theological studies at the Pontifical School of Theology affiliated with the Order's International

51

College at the foot of the Palatine on Via San Teodoro. During this time the College had a number of rectors, but the man who probably had the profoundest influence on young Kolbe was Father Stephen Ignudi. Genoese by birth but a Roman by inclination, he was thoroughly devoted to the pope and the rights of the Church, and was a staunch adversary of Freemasonry (meaning the anti-religious form of Freemasonry prevailing at the time in some European countries).

Msgr. Joseph Palatucci, Bishop of Campagna and one of Kolbe's fellow students at the International College, writes of Father Maximilian that "he oriented all his activities and works of devotion to Mary Immaculate, as means for the conversion of all the Church's enemies, and especially the Masons. Much of this can be explained by the fact that one of the rectors here was Father Stephen Ignudi, who, on both the occasions that he held this office, applied himself to forming us in an eminently Roman spirit, so that we became extremely loyal to the pope. He also imparted to us a spirit that was ready to go to war against every sort of evil, especially Freemasonry."

It is true that Maximilian Kolbe, in his devotion to the Immaculate, must have followed the trail blazed for him by the strong personality of Father Ignudi, but his first real "contact" with her, if I may use this expression, occurred two years before Ignudi assumed his rectorial duties at the International School. This moving and decisive encounter revealed his innocent candor and displayed his genuinely profound faith.

I speak of this as his *first* encounter with the Immaculate because, although he had been consecrated to Our Lady from childhood, he had lived in a country where, up until 1914, the Virgin had been venerated only under such aspects as Mother of God, Our Lady of Sorrows, and Queen of the Apostles. The Polish language had not yet found an adjective, equivalent to the Latin *immaculata*, to suitably express the privilege of Mary's immaculate conception.

But getting back to the actual incident: Friar Maximilian developed a very bad abscess on the thumb of his right hand, and when the school doctor saw all the pus that was forming, his verdict was inflexible: "Tomorrow we must amputate!"

Here was a heartbreaking prospect for one destined to become a priest. Now he would have to approach the altar of God to celebrate the Eucharist with a hand no longer able to handle the consecrated host in a proper way. But Friar Maximilian abandoned himself without complaint, or any words of reproach, to the will of God.

That same evening Father Bondini, at that time the rector, stopped by for a visit. "A long time ago," the rector told him, "I had much the same sort of difficulty. I must have been about twelve years old, but I remember screaming bloody murder from the pain it caused me. Mine was the same kind of abscess—a bone infection—but it was on my foot instead of my hand. My doctor also declared amputation necessary. He was a good doctor, professionally speaking, but an unbeliever if there ever was one.

"My mother was very much opposed to using the knife, naturally, but the doctor called some colleagues of his in for a consultation, and they all backed him up in his decision. As far as they could see, there was nothing to do but operate, and that as soon as possible—which meant the next day.

"But after the doctors left, my mother, with one of those rare impulses that only a mother can have, took my bandage off, washed my foot with soap, and covered it with a compress moistened with Lourdes water.

"Shortly afterwards I went to sleep, feeling no pain, and slept the night through. Next morning I knew right away I had been healed. When the doctor came to take me to surgery, my mother told him what had happened. He then started inveighing against what he called the superstitions of fanatics and the prattlings of peasants' children. But when he removed the bandage he saw a piece of rotted bone just ready to be ejected from the sole of my foot.

"He came up right away with some sort of scientific explanation, using some high-sounding terms, but it was quite evident he was just using the big words to play down the sudden, unexpected reversal of my illness. Sometime later I learned that this doctor was now so convinced of having seen a miracle take place, that he had become a Christian and had financed the building of a new church.

"I've told you what happened to me, and I guarantee it to be the truth. Now I happen to have here a bottle containing some Lourdes water. I'll leave it on your table."

Then he left. Next morning the school physician came to Friar Maximilian's room to prepare him for surgery.

"Doctor," the patient told him, "I believe I have here some medicine that could heal me without an operation. Would you please use it on me?"

After examining the bottle given him, the doctor needed no explanation, and, good Catholic that he was, he proceeded at once to make a compress, even though still doubtful that surgery could be avoided.

"Very well, then," he said, "we'll put everything off until tomorrow." And he left. But next day he was forced to admit that no operation would be necessary. After a little more medical treatment, the thumb was as good as new.

As I said, this was Kolbe's first encounter with Our Lady of Lourdes, and it was just after this that he became involved in incidents revealing his strong inclination toward apostolic work. He availed himself of every scrap of learning he had acquired, and every ounce of scientific ability, to break down the arguments of unbelievers, whom he willingly took on, whenever and wherever he met them, even on the train or in the streets.

One day in the center of Rome, for instance, Friar Maximilian heard a prominent politician sounding off with both barrels against the Church and the papacy. It was all the invitation he needed to dive head first into a discussion with the man, which he carried on with great fervor and telling accuracy. Finally, annoyed at seeing his entire arsenal of anticlerical guns turned against him, the pompous old fellow came back with: "That's enough out of you, kid! I ought to know what I'm talking about. After all, I have a degree in philosophy!"

"Well, so do I," said Friar Maximilian, and the other's eyes got as big as saucers, because this young friar hardly appeared to be more than sixteen years old. "But then," the man thought to himself, "a degree is a degree, and colleagues do have to respect one another."

So the dialogue continued—now on a more sophisticated level, but just as intensely—until at last the priest baiter found himself backed completely in a corner. Thereupon he fell silent, and seemed to be engaged in deep reflection. The description of this sparring match comes to us from Father Pal, who was an eyewitness.

On another occasion Friar Maximilian had gone with a fellow religious to see the Basilica of the Twelve Apostles and was returning to the school, when he came across a gang of teenagers engaged in a disgusting demonstration of disrespect for Our Lady. He broke into tears at once, and pushed his way into the center of their activities. "Why," he asked them between sobs, "why do you want to make the Blessed Virgin sad by acting this way?"

The boys vented all their sarcasm on him, the kind of sarcasm for which so many Romans are noted, replying that they "had to give someone a hard time anyway." Friar Maximilian's companion kept tugging at his sleeve, suggesting they clear out before the young gangsters got too excited. But Maximilian stood like Gibraltar, not giving in an inch. And he kept talking and arguing with them until he made every last one of them promise never to commit such blasphemies again. Only then was he ready to leave the scene.

Another time Friar Maximilian asked one of his companions in a very matter-of-fact way if he would accompany him to the Palazzo Verde, at that time the headquarters of Freemasonry. The young Pole had decided to beard the arch-lion in his den by trying to convert the Grand Master.

Kolbe had been deeply stirred by Father Ignudi's teaching and also by a disgusting spectacle he had witnessed in St. Peter's Square when the Masons were celebrating their bicentennial. The lodge members had held a noisy demonstration, waving banners that proclaimed: "Satan must reign in the Vatican, and the pope will be his slave." And they acted out sacrilegious parodies right under the pope's window. All this had inflamed the young Kolbe with the impatient desire to "do something."

His schoolmate consented to go along with the plan, but when they applied to the rector for permission, they could tell at once, from the indulgent smile he gave them, that their little project had run into a dead end.

"Of course, I myself would also like to see the Grand Master converted," the rector explained, "but I think what you have in mind is a little premature. Don't you think it would be better, for the present, to spend some time in prayer for the conversion of Masons?"

"Very well, then," Kolbe told his friend, "we shall begin our prayers at once," and headed straight for the chapel. That was typical of Maximilian Kolbe: immediate decisions in absolute obedience. For him there was no "tomorrow," but only "today," and no such thing as "gradually," but only "at once."

What we have seen thus far, however, was only the beginning. For during his Roman sojourn, this humble son of an enslaved Poland was to lay the groundwork for a movement of historical significance, not only for his own nation but for the entire world: the *Militia Immaculatae* (lit. "The troops of Mary Immaculate"), known today in North America as The Knights of the Immaculata Movement. This movement was destined to play an important role in the modern spiritual battles of the Church. More about that further on.

Here we will only add that on April 28, 1918, while the cannons of World War I were still blazing away on many fronts, Maximilian Kolbe was ordained a priest at Sant'Andrea della Valle. Next day he celebrated his first Mass at Sant'Andrea delle Fratte, on the Altar of the Miracle, where in 1842 the Virgin is said to have appeared to a certain Alphonse Ratisbonne, transforming that "ferocious wolf" into a gentle lamb.

Fifteen months later, Father Maximilian returned to Poland, having just received his diploma in theology. The roll at the Franciscan College retains to this day a terse entry (number 277) made by the hand of Father Stephen Ignudi, summarizing Kolbe's residence at Rome: "Maximilian Kolbe, province of Galicia; arrived October 29, 1912; ordained to the priesthood, April 28, 1918; degree in philosophy from Pontifical Gregorian University; degree in sacred theology from this College, July 22, 1919; departed July 23, 1919. A young saint."

4

Beginnings

Auschwitz, August 14, 1941. The infirmary telephone rang. They were looking for Doctor Boch.

The white-gowned physician stood frozen at attention with the receiver at his ear, listening impassively. At the end of the conversation he merely said, *"Jawohl!"* and went at once to a glass cabinet whose shelves were lined with instruments. Opening the door, he removed four syringes equipped with slanted tips, such as are used for intravenous injections. In each he inserted a sterilized needle.

Next, he went to a rack where several beakers were arranged in meticulous order, bearing a variety of labels and containing liquids of different colors. Taking the large stopper from a container marked "Phenol," he inserted the needle of each syringe into the clear liquid, carefully maneuvering the piston to obtain a full cylinder.

Holding the bundle of syringes in his left hand, with his right hand he reached for a red rubber hemostat. Banging the rubber hose against his leg, like a horseman trying out his whip, he left the infirmary and headed for the Starvation Bunker, where Father Maximilian Kolbe had not yet succumbed to his slow death.

It was incredible: after so many days without so much as a crumb of bread or a drop of water, lying stark naked in the dense, putrid darkness of an underground cell, sealed off from the world by an iron door, after months of suffering under the tyranny of SS overlords, months of exhausting work under the forced labor program, Father Maximilian Kolbe, his lungs riddled with tuberculosis, was still alive!

During those terrible days he had seen one after another of his nine companions succumb to this horrifying punishment imposed by the Lagerführer on innocent hostages as retribution for one prisoner's escape. "At the end," says the sole witness, Bruno Borgowiec, "only four men remained alive, and among them Father Kolbe."

But for several days the other three survivors had lain, unresponsive, on the cold cement floor, mere skeletons completely eaten away by the ferocity of their own hunger, their chests vibrating almost imperceptibly with the last feeble stirrings of life.

Father Maximilian had bidden each one a tender farewell before they sank into unconsciousness, just as he had done for those already taken to

61

the crematorium. With a look of serenity he had imprinted upon their faces the image of his own attractive smile, accompanying them to the very threshold of eternity, praying fervently to the Immaculate, his Mamusia. Now he knew for certain that she was also about to call him, to present him at last with that red crown she had offered him so long ago in the faraway church in Pabianice, near Lodz, when he was a child.

No doubt about it now: his time had come. For the last few days he had not been able to stand, or even to kneel. He could only sit with his back supported against the rough wall, his face turned toward the iron door.

So many days, and it wasn't over yet! "At this point," says Borgowiec, "the authorities decided the affair had been prolonged long enough. The cell was now needed for other victims." A new contingent of innocent victims, chosen according to the Lagerführer's whimsical procedure, awaited their turn in the torture chamber.

This was why the infirmary telephone had rung and Doctor Boch had proceeded with a *"Jawohl"* to prepare his tools of death. This was why he was headed for the Bunker, brandishing his red rubber hemostat like a horseman's whip.

Doctor Boch, the white-coated executioner, the scientist who always answered *"Jawohl!"* and carried out the sentence with a syringe full of carbolic acid, was on his way to Father Maximilian's cell. It was the 14th of August 1941, vigil of the Assumption, of the day commemorating Mamusia's entrance through the gates of heaven....

Maximilian Kolbe was still in Rome, pursuing his theological studies at the Franciscan International College on Via San Teodoro, and World War I was in full swing, when he founded the *Militia Immaculatae.*

Various talented writers have provided us with fine accounts of this important event. But I know none of them will feel slighted if, after having read them, I have chosen to present here the simplest account of all, written with the utmost humility and economy of words, set down by its author almost unwillingly, solely out of obedience to the one who had assigned him the task.

The author is Maximilian Kolbe himself, who penned the story in 1935 in response to the request of his Guardian, Father Florian Koziura, for a brief description of the origin of the M.I.

"Much has happened since then," Kolbe begins. "It has been about eighteen years, and I may have forgotten quite a few details. But since Father Guardian has ordered me to describe the beginnings of the M.I., I'll just tell what I can remember....

"Well, I remember as a small boy buying a little statue of Our Lady for five kopeks. Later, while a student at Lwów, I prostrated myself before the high altar and promised the Blessed Virgin, seated like a queen above her altar, that I would be her soldier. I wasn't sure, actually, how I would keep my promise, but I thought in terms of combating with material arms."

Kolbe seems to refer here to that vocational crisis that came upon him on the eve of his entry into the novitiate.

"Then, just before entering the novitiate (or just before being professed; I don't really remember) I shared my problems with my prefect, the late Father Denis Sowiak, who commuted my vow to take up arms into an obligation to recite daily the prayer *Sub Tuum Praesidium,* a practice that has continued to the present, even though now I know quite well what kind of battles the Immaculate had in mind for me."

So we see that the Immaculate had ordered him to fight for her. At first he hadn't understood what this warfare was all about, but neither had Francis of Assisi quite understood in his youth the immense significance of the divine command: "Arise, and repair my house that is in ruins." St. Francis immediately began making a stockpile of large stones to use in restoring the little church of St. Damian. There is a refreshing promptness in this obedience of the saints. They begin carrying out an order at once, and to the letter.

"Repair my house," said Christ, and Francis of Assisi became a stonemason. "Go to war for me," said the Virgin, and Maximilian decides to enlist in the army. Neither of these, in their radical humility, could have then imagined the vast implications of the heavenly command.

"Despite my strong inclination to pride,"

Father Maximilian continues, "I felt a great attraction to the Immaculate.... In my cell, above the place where I knelt for prayer, I always kept the likeness of some saint to whom the Bless Virgin had appeared. I would also invoke this saint frequently, and eventually some fellow religious would notice this and remark that I must surely have a great devotion for 'such and such a saint.'"

Actually, for Maximilian the picture of "such and such a saint" was intended as a constant reminder of the Blessed Virgin's apparition to himself as a child, when she had offered him the two crowns. But even here he was not about to divulge that secret.

"As the Masons began demonstrating with ever-increasing arrogance, waving their black banners which depicted Lucifer treading the Archangel Michael underfoot, and distributing tracts and booklets that attacked the Holy Father, the idea occurred to me of founding an association to oppose the Masons and other satanic forces....

"In the meantime," he says, "we went to take a vacation at La Vigna, less than half an hour's walk from the International College. One day, during a game of soccer, I tasted blood in my mouth. I stole away from the playing field and stretched myself out on the grass in a nearby meadow. The late Friar Jerome Biasi looked after me."

This was the first telltale showing of blood indicating pulmonary tuberculosis. The symptoms were to reappear fairly often thereafter in Father

65

Maximilian's life. But, with the exception of Biasi, none of his fellow students was aware of the problem.

True, one of his fellow religious remembers "the redness over his cheekbones and his eternally cold hands—like cakes of ice in the wintertime." And another recalls that Kolbe often suffered from severe headaches, but he adds that even this difficulty was known only to the rector and a few of the priests. "As for me, I could tell when he was suffering because of the contractions of his facial muscles."

But none of his associates had the least suspicion that he was tubercular—only Friar Biasi, who a short time later carried Kolbe's secret with him to the grave. Here was something he had learned from the living example of Father Venance, that ailing saint he had come to know in Lwów, and who had demonstrated how a Franciscan could observe the Rule conscientiously under the most trying conditions, concealing his physical suffering beneath the most radiant of smiles.

Father Maximilian continues: "For some time I continued to spit up blood, and I was actually happy, because I thought this might be the end! Afterward I went to a doctor, and he told me to get back to Via San Teodoro and go to bed. But the treatment seemed to have little effect in stopping the continual hemorrhages. Friar Jerome Biasi came to see me often in those days....

"Two weeks later my doctor let me out of bed. Accompanied by Father Ossana, I returned to our house in the country. But I was so weak I could hardly make it. My schoomates, I remember, were so glad to see me that they shouted for joy, and they brought me fresh figs, bread, and wine. . . .

"Now the pains were gone and there were no more hemorrhages. It was then that, for the first time, I confided my idea of founding an association to Friar Jerome Biasi and Father Joseph Pal, who was already ordained, even though he was my classmate in theology. I made everything conditional on their securing permission from their spiritual directors, which was to be a test of God's will in this matter.

"As soon as I had become a little stronger they sent me to Viterbo for a little extra vacation. I was accompanied by Friar Anthony Glowinski, and on that occasion he too became a member of the *Militia.* Soon afterward we were joined by the late Friar Anthony Mansi and by Friar Henry Granata of the Neapolitan Province.

"Outside of these actual participants in the *Militia,* no one at the College knew of its existence except the rector, Father Stephen Ignudi. We always kept him informed of everything, and did nothing without his permission, for the will of the Immaculate always manifests itself through obedience.

"Thus on October 16, 1917, with our rector's permission we held our first meeting, at which seven members were present: Father Joseph Pal, a priest of the Rumanian Province; Father Anthony Glowinski, who died in 1918 in the Rumanian

Province; Friar Jerome Biasi of the Paduan Province, died 1929; Father Quiricus Pignalberi, Roman Province; Friar Anthony Mansi; Friar Henry Granata, Neapolitan Province; myself."

Father Maximilian thus places himself at the tail end of his list of seven "founders" (three Slavs and four Italians). But he, of course, was the real, the only founder of the M.I. The others were his charter members, the first little squad of what was to become a great army.

"Our meeting was held in the evening hours, a secret gathering behind the closed doors of an inner chamber. In front of us stood a little statue of the Immaculate and two burning candles. Friar Jerome Biasi acted as secretary. The order of business was to outline a program for the M.I., something in writing to explain its purpose, especially since Father Alexander Basile, confessor to the Holy Father, had promised to ask the Pope for his blessing on the M.I. That promise was never kept, but we managed to receive a papal blessing anyway, from Pope Benedict XV, which was transmitted to us orally on March 26, 1919, by a member of our Order, Bishop Dominic Jaquet, at that time a professor of Church history at our College."

Father Kolbe, as you can see, draws us a very rough picture of this historic occasion, not dwelling on any detail, and keeping himself very much in the background. But some additional information, worth mentioning, is available from Father Joseph Pal: "On the evening of October 16, 1917, in anticipation of the feast of St. Margaret Mary Alacoque on the 17th, Friar Maximilian Kolbe called us to a meeting in a room adjoining that of the rector and read to us from a small sheet of paper the program he had worked out on his own, and which has since been published and become well known under the title: *Militia Immaculatae*. He asked us if we approved it and requested us to sign it. As a priest and the oldest, I was the first to subscribe. I believe Friar Maximilian was the last to affix his name. I'm not sure if this original document is still preserved at the first headquarters of the M.I. It would make an interesting item of evidence, showing how Friar Maximilian, not the least bit concerned with outward formalities, used about one eighth of a sheet of notebook paper to write the charter of such a tremendous work of piety and apostolic action.

"From our meeting room we then proceeded to the college chapel, where unknown to anyone but ourselves, I blessed the medal and bestowed it on myself, Friar Maximilian, and the other charter members of the Immaculate's army. Then, quietly, we stole away, each to his own cell. Of those not actually present, only Father Rector knew of it. The foundations of the M.I. had been laid."

Here we have Father Pal's version of the story. As for the organizational charter, written on a scrap of paper, this was found among some of Maximilian Kolbe's private papers, secretly collected and preserved by Father Quiricus Pignalberi as precious remembrances.

The document, drawn up in very simple Latin, reads as follows:

"She shall crush your head" (Gen. 3, 15).
"You alone [Mary] have crushed all heresies in the whole world" [Former Office of the Blessed Virgin Mary.]

I. Purpose
Pursue the conversion of every person living in sin, heresy, schism and especially Freemasonry, and the growth in holiness of all persons, under the sponsorship of the Blessed Virgin Mary Immaculate.

II. Conditions
1. Make a voluntary and total oblation of oneself to the Blessed Virgin Mary Immaculate as an instrument in her most holy hands.
2. Carry or wear the "Miraculous Medal."

III. Means
1. Once a day if possible, beseech the Immaculate with the ejaculation: "O Mary conceived without sin, pray for us who have recourse to you, and for all who do not have recourse to you especially for the Freemasons."
2. Use all the legitimate means that one's particular state in life, condition, and varying opportunities make possible, the

choice of which is left to the zeal and
prudence of each member, and especially,
propagate the "Miraculous Medal."

Here is an undoubtedly inspiring, yet disturbing, document. To the skeptical, knowing eyes of a
worldling, it might even seem absurd. A prayer and
a medal—to bring about the conversion, even the
sanctification, of half of humanity! Seen with such
eyes it might easily remind us of some episode from
our childhood when we formed a secret club and
wrote down the rules in code. All we needed was a
password, a bow and arrow made from a couple of
branches and a piece of string, and we were ready to
conquer the world!

But time has shown that the disbelieving,
know-it-all eyes of the world simply cannot grasp
certain aspects of reality. For it was precisely these
three key points jotted down by young Maximilian
Kolbe that would form the basis of a vast religious
movement, a crusade in defense of Christianity,
under the banner of Mary Immaculate. Today more
than two million people all over the world are
affiliated with the M.I. and they have been able to
penetrate Marian dogma and privilege so deeply
that they have found in them the antidote for all the
forces of evil which openly or secretly are waging
war against the sovereignty of Christ and of his
Church.

Yet the first steps taken by the crusade were
anything but world-shaking. Kolbe comments, in

fact, that "for an entire year following that first meeting, the M.I. made practically no progress and encountered such obstacles as to discourage even the charter members, who did not dare to speak of it any more. One of them, in fact, even made it his business to convince his comrades of its uselessness.... Then it happened that Father Anthony Glowinski and Friar Anthony Mansi were struck down by the Spanish influenza, and within thirteen days of each other they died and went to be with the Immaculate.

"I also suffered a relapse of my lung condition, coughing a lot and spitting up blood. Excused from my studies, I made use of the time to recopy the M.I.'s charter, so that I could submit it to the Father General of our Order, Father Dominic Tavani, and ask for his blessing upon it in writing. When I did so, he said 'If only there were at least twelve of you!...' Nonetheless he gave his blessing on April 14, 1919, in writing, and expressed his desire that the M.I. might be spread among the youth. From that day on there was a steady flow of new members.

The actual activity of the M.I. during this initial period consisted in private prayer and the distribution of medals of the Immaculate Conception, popularly called 'the Miraculous Medal.' Even Father General contributed some money for the purchase of these medals."

Perhaps no one, least of all Maximilian, would have thought that in just a few years the M.I. would have founded two cities, one in Poland and one in Japan. The first was called Niepokalanów (Nye-po-kah-lah'-noof) meaning "City of the Immaculate," and the second, Mugenzai No Sono, a more poetical Japanese equivalent—literally "Garden of the Immaculate." And probably no one could have dreamed that Poland, Japan, and other countries would be invaded by this same M.I. in the form of daily newspapers and large circulation magazines.

No, not even Maximilian could have foreseen it, but unwittingly he was preparing for it by patterning his life after the Rule of St. Francis, while at the same time opening heart and mind to every new advance in science and technology. His was a fully optimistic, solidly grounded belief in the goodness of human progress, because he saw the possibilities of converting the fruits of such progress into a formidable arsenal of weapons to be used for the glory of God. While a large segment of the Catholic world still looked with great suspicion upon these human conquests of nature, Maximilian saw that they must be appropriated and vigorously applied to the cause of righteousness.

The power of the printed word, for example, was something he was fully aware of, and during his college days he dreamed of someday founding a periodical that would be the means of instructing all the world's peoples in the Gospel, under the patronage of Mary Immaculate. His own words several years later reveal his heart's desire: "The earth needs to be flooded with a mighty deluge of

Christian and Marian literature, written in every language and reaching every country, so as to drown in the waves of truth all those voices of error that have been using the printing press as their most powerful ally. The globe must be encircled by words of life in printed form, so that the world may once again experience the joy of living."

He was also among the very first Catholics to realize—in 1917, when the movie era began—that the invention of the moving picture offered extraordinary possibilities for good. While others at the Franciscan College in Rome were worrying about those films of dubious morality that were then claiming public attention—even defining the cinema itself as "a tool of perdition" and organizing a campaign for its suppression—Friar Maximilian calmly told a schoolmate very much heated up over the controversy, "No, I disagree. The movie was meant to benefit society. Our job is to get it moving in that direction."

His friend was scandalized. "How can you say such a thing? Don't you know that the devil and his followers always take over new inventions and scientific advances and exploit them for evil purposes?"

"Then that's all the more reason for us to finally wake up, get to work, and take back the positions our enemy has occupied," young Kolbe told him.

In July 1919, Father Maximilian, an ordained priest with degrees in philosophy and theology, arrived in Cracow, feeling he could hardly wait to get his M.I. on the firing line. He found a bleeding, devastated Poland, a free nation now, but with an empty treasury, an economy on the brink of ruin, her citizens involved in a desperate struggle to ward off what seemed like an impending catastrophe. For their ailing nation the people donated their prized family heirlooms, and submitted to the most rigorous economic restraints.

But despite such heroic sacrifices, the storm of inflation broke relentlessly upon them, spreading disaster. The price of a kilogram of lard skyrocketed until it was as much as that of a two-story house. Then the newspaper headlines announced the advance of the Red Army from the east. Although "the miracle of the Vistula" halted the Soviet invasion, soon a new cause of death made the headlines: dreadful epidemics of influenza were practically depopulating the eastern provinces.

Cracow was about the worst place to live for anyone who suffered from lung disease, and Maximilian had already had his first bout with tuberculosis. In fact his fellow Franciscan, Father Kubit, states that Father Kolbe arrived in Cracow "weak and sickly" and with little hope of being able to do much work.

Yet despite everything they made him a teacher. The flu epidemic had so reduced the ranks of priests and religious, already made scarce by the war, that every new recruit simply had to be pressed into service.

These were the circumstances under which Father Maximilian Kolbe began his campaign. His first objective was to impart to his fellow friars his own enthusiasm and then to enlist them in the work of the Immaculate.

He was bitterly disillusioned. The only response he got was a shrug of the shoulders, and he earned himself a couple of new nicknames. Now they called him "Dreamer" and "Nuisance." *"Ecce somniator venit"* ("Here comes that dreamer!") was the refrain that stifled any attempt he might have made to speak.

And all this was only a foreshadowing of what was to be characteristic of his whole lifework: physical suffering, disappointments, opposition, and even ridicule. But this was only evidence to him that his M.I. was the work of God, for all God's works need the cross in order to grow and blossom.

5

These Troublesome Saints

Auschwitz, August 14, 1941. Doctor Boch descended the dark stairway to the Starvation Bunker, the four intravenous syringes in his left hand, the red rubber hemostat in his right. A couple of hard-stepping SS men went ahead of him, while bringing up the rear was the indispensable Bruno Borgowiec, not serving for the moment as interpreter or stenographer, but merely as the undertaker of Block 13.

The big key turned stiffly in the lock and the iron door swung open, allowing the beam of light from an electric lantern to enter and dispel the darkness, revealing a spectacle of slow death.

There sat Father Maximilian Kolbe, naked, a living skeleton. He occupied the same position he had assumed three days earlier, his head inclined slightly to the left, a gentle smile on his lips. His hands lay helpless in his lap, and his back was propped up against the wall.

The other three emaciated victims of hunger and thirst lay sprawled out on the floor, unconscious but still alive. Doctor Boch moved coolly, dispassionately toward the four who had survived the prolonged torture. With one knee on the floor, he applied the rubber hemostat to the first unconscious prisoner's left arm, stuck a needle into his vein, released the rubber hose, and pushed the piston of the syringe forward. The same operation was repeated on the other two prostrate men, and each time the phenol had completed its work before the needle was ever pulled out of the vein.

Now it was Kolbe's turn. The white-gowned executioner rose to his feet and headed in his direction. "Then with a prayer on his lips, Father Kolbe held out his arm to the executioner," says Bruno Borgowiec. "It was too much for me; I didn't want to see it. So I mumbled some excuse about having to do some work in the office, and fled from the scene."

Going back twenty-two years to July 1919, we find Maximilian Kolbe returning from Rome a priest, to a Poland now free and unoccupied by foreigners, but left in turmoil by the war, devastated by the effects of inflation, under attack by the Soviet army, and its population decimated by the flu epidemic.

Kolbe's health was very poor, but the grave national situation necessitated that everyone give their utmost. So he was assigned to teach Church history at the Franciscan seminary in Cracow. He threw himself into the work with all he had, but tuberculosis had by now so damaged both his lungs that he had to lecture in a very low voice—so low, in fact, that not many of the students could follow what he had to say.

Within two months his superiors had to relieve him of his teaching duties. He was now relegated to a parish church, where his duties consisted of hearing confessions and preaching short sermons. But the time he spent in the confessional was actually harder on his lungs than the classroom work. And the scarcity of food in the country, felt at the Cracow friary as much as anywhere, added the finishing touches to Kolbe's plight.

Every step Father Maximilian took, every gesture he made, had to be executed with painful slowness. A single overexertion could set off a hemorrhage, and this was something that, under the circumstances, could have been extremely serious.

Surprisingly, all this suffering—which occasioned his inaudible voice and his ridiculously slow movements—instead of exciting sympathy, only provoked ridicule. Few of his fellow religious discerned anything of the tragedy behind his peculiar behavior—known only to a few of the administrators—and were not capable of penetrating behind that bitter-sweet, submissive smile and patient docility to see the sharpness of his ingenuity and his extraordinarily vivacious personality. Thus a few jokers (even seminaries seem to have them) amused themselves by feigning to talk in the same weak voice and caricaturing the provocative slowness of his movements, thus lending credence to the opinion of some that this professor who had come from Rome and had only lasted two months on the job was perhaps a little deficient in the upper story.

The trouble with this simpleton was that he was such a bore, never missing a chance to buttonhole someone and talk his ear off—with that almost inaudible voice of his—always on the subject of his M.I. and the need to enlist in it, to help launch a crusade, etc. "The poor man has a fixation. He's just a crazy nuisance!"

Yes, like it or not, saints are always uncomfortable to have around. They are so different from everyone else! And besides, they have a way of disturbing our everyday existence—perhaps, as in this instance, with a voice that is barely audible and movements that are awkward, even ridiculous; but definitely, in every instance, in ways that are unwelcome and inopportune. They are flies in the ointment, square pegs in a sea of round holes. Their very presence almost forces us to examine our conscience, which is, of course, precisely what we least desire to do. They are such a nuisance!

So up come our banners of resistance. We smile condescendingly at them, and give them names that are really a cover-up for our defensive attitude. They have a mania, a fixation, delusions of grandeur, a tendency to oversimplify, a touch of madness, etc. What a variety of "definitions" we can choose from! Thus we barricade ourselves behind our masks of scorn, hoping to gain a little time before we must make that inevitable examination of conscience.

But it would be a great mistake to think that Maximilian Kolbe lightheartedly accepted all this shrugging of shoulders, this smirking and burlesquing. It caused him immense suffering—much more than did the disease that was inexorably eating away his lungs.

But he never betrayed those feelings. Not once did he lay aside his smile or allow his personal pride to take over. Even "Sister Suffering" must be made welcome, he felt, and he was convinced that "we will accomplish much more if we are immersed in exterior and interior darkness, filled with sadness, deprived of consolations, persecuted relentlessly, constantly surrounded by failures, deserted by everyone, ridiculed, scoffed at as much as Jesus was on the cross—provided that meanwhile we pray with all our might for those who persecute us, and seek by every means to bring them to God and Mary Immaculate.

So he clenched his teeth, and prayed, and continued to make a nuisance of himself among his fellow friars and students, until he found some who did not consider him a nuisance.

We have noted already that the beginning of the M.I. can be traced to that clandestine evening meeting on October 16, 1917, in an inner chamber of the Franciscan International College on Via San

Teodoro in Rome, when seven young men became the charter members. But there is another date in the history of the M.I. that is possibly just as important.

Kolbe has this entry: "Tuesday, October 7, 1919, feast of Our Lady of the Holy Rosary. During free time this evening, six seminarians, together with their rector, Father Keller, signed their names in a book that will serve as the membership roll for the M.I. Because of my earlier membership in the Roman Militia, they asked me to affix my signature first. My dear Mamusia, I don't know where this affair is headed, but may you be pleased to dispose of me and the others as you care to, and for the greater glory of God. My Mamusia, my Immaculate Mother, I belong to you. You know how miserable I am, how close I walk to the brink of the precipice, and how much I am plagued with love of myself. Should your spotless hands cease to support me, I would fall, first into the gravest of sins and then into the depths of hell. But if, unworthy as I am, you do not leave me, and if you guide me, then I shall surely not fall, but become a great saint."

So then, Father Kolbe had no idea *where* the M.I. was headed, but he foresaw quite well *what* the M.I. was to become. Though born out of the spirit of St. Francis and ever loyal to its Franciscan origins, it was destined to outgrow the Order itself. Likewise, it was not to remain a mere devotional confraternity, but was to become a movement and, as such, attract the masses of people and penetrate all the various lay associations, as well as the religious orders, congregations and institutes, providing something that would complement every vocation and bring each one to the highest flowering of sainthood.

After that eventful October 7, things started moving, and fast. On October 22, the provincial, Father Louis Karwacki, gave his blessing to the undertaking. Less than two months later, Father Maximilian was received at the bishop's residence, where he briefed Bishop Sapieha of Cracow on the beginnings of the M.I., explained its program of action, and asked permission to publish its bylaws. Just a few days later the episcopal permission arrived, and his provincial authorized the distribution of M.I. literature.

"Now we begin our work!" said Father Kolbe, and begin he did, working wonders with his feeble voice during a week of meetings held in the Italian Room of the Cracow friary. His listeners included both men and women, young and old, priests, religious, and lay people.

"Sometimes," he told a gathering of seminarians, "the best of our intentions are interpreted in a bad light. Sometimes they actually give rise to evil reports about us. Persecution does not always come from our enemies, but also from good, pious persons, saintly people who may even be enrolled in the M.I. Perhaps we can know no greater sorrow than to see such as these blocking the road in front of us, while having every intention of giving glory to God. How it pains us to see them tearing down what we have built up, and striving to alienate the souls of others from us.

"Nevertheless, though everything be against us, there remains for us one lesson, one compass that we can depend on: holy obedience, in which is always manifested the will of the Immaculate. My superiors can be mistaken, but I shall never be mistaken by obeying them. If obedience tells me 'yes' today and tomorrow 'no,' then today I will obey the 'yes' and tomorrow the 'no' and never claim that I have been deceived."

At the conclusion of his week of meetings, Maximilian brought together all those who had enrolled up to that point, for an inaugural session of the M.I., in which he proposed the idea of "Marian focus groups" and outlined the bases on which they were to operate. The first of these focus groups were begun without delay among university students, young women studying at religious institutes, and soldiers stationed in Cracow.

At once the need arose for a way to maintain contact and unity between the individual members of the M.I., who came from such a variety of social backgrounds and who worked in such different settings, as well as among the focus groups which were operating in very diverse environments. Maximilian knew immediately that this meant publishing a magazine, and decided that the name of this magazine would be: *Rycerz Niepokalanej (The Knight of the Immaculate)*.

But just at this critical moment all his extraordinary exertions caught up with him, and he suffered a complete physical collapse. His temperature soared to 104°, and suddenly everyone began discovering what disease he had been suffering from. "And no one went to see him," writes Brother Bombrys, "perhaps for fear of catching the disease."

So he remained alone in bed in his little cell, lying on a sweat-impregnated straw mattress that caved in uncomfortably at the center. On the chest of drawers in front of him he had a statue of his Mamusia, and on the old desk in the corner were pictures of St. Theresa of the Child Jesus and Saint Gemma Galgani.

Eventually his condition grew so much worse that his superiors decided to send him to one of the sanatoriums at Zakopane. Zakopane was noted for its anticlerical atmosphere, a condition that thrived there because of the absence of any religious personnel, this vacuum being deliberately cultivated by the secularists who ran some of the various institutions.

Father Maximilian remained at Zakopane from August 1920 till April 1921, after which he was sent to the sanatorium at Nieszawa where he remained until December 1921. "All our trials," he had told his listeners at a meeting in Cracow, "are very useful and necessary to us, I might even say indispensable, because they are the crucible in which the gold of our lives is purified."

At Zakopane he went from one hemorrhage to another, then alternated between improvements and relapses, then found, at last, some relief, if not an absolute cure, from a process known as "pneumothorax." At any rate, he was feeling well enough to undertake an "expedition" against what was considered the impregnable stronghold of atheism at Zakopane: the hospital operated by a university mutual aid association.

Of the many university students who were patients at this hospital, only one girl called herself a Catholic. All the rest styled themselves "free thinkers." Maximilian began spending quite a bit of time in the hospital corridors, or on the verandas where the young people rested in their deck chairs, or else he walked the paths where patients took their exercise. He was so adept at using his lively intellect, his breadth of cultural interests, and his attractive smile, that it was not long before some of these students had invited him to hold some meetings.

"You understand, don't you, Father? This sanatorium life gets so boring after a while that...."

"I know what you mean. And don't worry. I'll be glad to join the fight against boredom."

By the time the first meeting was over, some of the "towers of strength" began to feel a little shaky already about their own powers of resistance, and from then on they stayed away, afraid to "run the risk." But those who were more sure of their own opinions stayed on, in order to hear what he had to say. In a few days' time four of the most aggressive freethinkers were converted, and wanted everyone to know about it. From then on, there was a small but steady stream of confessions.

Father Kolbe noticed that one of his most attentive listeners was a student from Tarnów, a clean-out young man with an intelligent look in his eyes. He was sure this fellow would be among the first converts, but nothing happened. After every meeting he went away at once, without so much as a backward glance. Then one day he didn't.

"At last!" thought Maximilian, and his heart beat faster with joy. But the young man had only come to tell him good-bye, because this was the last meeting he could attend. His condition was becoming so hopeless that from now on he would not be able to leave his bed, and death was just around the corner.

He took time to ask the young man some questions, and found that he was of the Jewish race and religion. "I'll come to see you," Kolbe told him.

"Impossible, Father. No one is allowed to visit a patient in critical condition."

"But I'll come anyway." And come he did, even if he had to do it when no one was looking. He was present during the young man's last hours on earth, and at his request he baptized him, gave him Communion and administered the Sacrament of the Sick. Then he hung a Miraculous Medal around his neck. In the young man's eyes he could read an infinite joy, but he also detected a slight shadow— "Tell me what's bothering you, son."

"My mother. My mother is coming here, and she's a fanatical Jewess."

"Don't worry. You'll be in heaven before she gets here."

The student breathed his last at 11 a.m. The mother arrived at noon. The first thing she saw was not the serene smile on the dead boy's face but the medal of Our Lady. With a loud cry, she tore it off his body, and for a few minutes the whole sanatorium could hear her screams. "You've robbed me of my son, and killed him, as well!"

She made such a scene that doctors, nurses and patients all came running, followed quickly by the hospital administrator, who glared at Maximilian and pointed toward the exit. "Get out of here, and don't set foot in here again!"

"I'm terribly sorry, sir, but I plan to come here during visiting hours, just like anyone else." And that is what he did, and arranged with the students for an entire series of talks defending the existence of God and the divinity of Jesus.

Finally, his lungs now improved as much as could be expected, he returned to Cracow, determined to take up "Operation Immaculata" at the point where he had left it when he fell ill: the planning of a periodical as a means of liaison within the movement. Upon his return, the Italian Room of the friary began bulging at the seams with a flock of new members for the M.I. And so he went to see the provinicial with his plans.

"It's a perfectly good idea, Father Maximilian, to put out this bulletin," he told him, "but only on condition that you raise the necessary funds yourself, because the community here is too poor to help you."

Raise the money yourself! Easily said, of

course; but how do you go about it? One solution he kept dismissing as impossible, but finally adopted: begging for the money.

Beginning in a low-rent neighborhood, he turned around and headed for home three times before getting up enough courage to knock on the first door. And when he actually knocked and someone came to the door, he blushed to the very roots of his hair, so great was his embarrassment at the idea of begging.

But eventually he collected enough (and only from the poorest families) to begin his project. Thus in January 1922, just when the general financial crisis was forcing well-established papers and magazines out of business, the first edition of *The Knight of the Immaculate* appeared, paid for by the offerings of the poor and put together almost entirely by one obscure man—Father Maximilian himself. An honest little insertion in the masthead warned the reading public that "due to a lack of funds, the regular appearance of this review cannot be guaranteed." Probably no publication was ever launched on such a slender "shoe-string" as this one, looking at it from a purely commercial standpoint.

The expenses for the second issue were also raised by begging, and then Father Maximilian discovered, when the periodical had already gone to press, that there had been a devaluation of the currency since the first issue, so that all the money he had collected for the second was practically worthless.

What next? At this point he appealed to his

guardian (as superiors of Franciscan communities are called), who told him: "You see what happens, when you bite off more than you can chew? You'll have to get out of this the best way you can, and without getting the friary involved."

Father Maximilian left the superior's room with a feeling of dismay. All he had was the money he had begged, and it wouldn't pay the bill.

He headed for the church to pray for help before Our Lady's altar. As he was praying, he noticed an envelope on the altar. On it was written, "For you, my Immaculate Mother." Inside he found a considerable sum of money, the exact amount he needed to pay the printer.

Throughout the ensuing development of the *Knight,* Father Maximilian always asserted that the magazine's success could not be explained in purely human terms. Its writing was plain, its early layout poor. It had been launched with money received in charitable donations during a time when the national economy was hopelessly un-stable. Yet its initial survival and later growth would defy all the laws of economics, with utter disregard for predictions based on "common sense" or other human criteria. When anyone asked Kolbe about its success, he would just say, "I guess that is a secret the Immaculate keeps to herself."

Rather ambitiously, and with the Immaculate's help, 5,000 copies of both the first and second issues were printed and distributed. And from then on, with her continuing assistance, Kolbe and his growing number of collaborators succeeded in

90

maintaining this output every month, without fail, for the next two years, after which the *Knight* began its spectacular growth (reaching a circulation of 800,000 in 1938).

But, of course, there were difficulties. First among these were rising costs, which caused Kolbe to change printers several times in the first six months. In addition there were a series of strikes in the printing trades which necessitated further changes.

As a result, Maximilian began thinking seriously about acquiring a printing press. When he mentioned this to Father Guardian, the poor man heaved a long sigh. "Well, go ahead. But, mind you, I don't want to hear anything about money. You have to take care of that yourself!"

Father Guardian, unfortunately, was caught between two fires. On the one hand, he didn't want to throw a wet blanket on Kolbe's initiative and enthusiasm, but at the same time he had to reckon with a difficult situation shaping up in his community.

With that "crazy" Father Maximilian coming and going at all hours, busy with his M.I., and with his magazine always on the verge of bankruptcy, life in the peaceful old friary was definitely not the same anymore. Some of the friars felt that their whole world was about to collapse, that an entire tradition was being upset, that a whole way of thinking, of living, of reaching sanctity was being turned upside down.

"We don't see anything of the spirit of St.

Francis in an enterprise that publishes magazines. Our job is to hear confessions and preach. Then we can still pray in peace." Thus spoke some of the ancient fathers of the community, forgetting, of course, that in the days of St. Francis there were no printing presses yet. In his days there were no trains either, yet these same friars seemed ready enough to use such modern means of transportation—not to mention cars and airplanes, which in cases of necessity they felt it was quite all right to use instead of St. Francis' faithful donkey!

Just when the cussing and discussing of Kolbe's proposal to buy a press had reached its peak, a fellow friar arrived from the United States. This was Father Lawrence Cyman, who, on a tour through Poland, stopped over at Cracow. During recreation some of the fathers started blowing off steam to their visitor about the trouble in their community, and showed him copies of the magazine.

"See how badly it's printed? And the literary quality is no better.... What a fuss he makes over it!... Father Maximilian thinks he's going to convert the whole world with this thing!...And that's not all. Now he wants to have his own printing press!...And he doesn't have a penny in his pocket!...But to compensate for that he's head over heels in debt!"

Father Maximilian was on hand to hear all these wonderful compliments, and kept his eyes on the ground so that no one could see him blushing with embarrassment.

"Well, now," said Father Cyman, "I don't see anything wrong at all with wanting to get a printing press. If I were in his shoes, I would do the same thing. I don't see why you make such a joke of it. And just to get things started, I promise you a down payment, Father: one hundred dollars!"

A few days later Father Kolbe went to call on the Sisters of Mercy at Lagiewniki, who possessed a press of venerable vintage which they wished to sell. When at last he emerged from his visit, it was all settled: now the Immaculate would have her printing press.

"That does it!" said the old-timers. "As if it wasn't enough disturbance having those M.I. people streaming in and out of here. Now we'll have the noise of machinery as well. Who knows what it will be next!"

Then someone had an inspiration that was to prove providential for all concerned. Since Father Kolbe's tuberculosis was only arrested and not cured, wouldn't the climate of Grodno, on the other side of Poland, be better for his health? The air was wonderful, over there in the east. Just the thing for weak lungs!

When Father Maximilian and his dinosaur of a printing press arrived in Grodno, he found a very run-down friary but a sympathetic superior who showed himself at once to be not only interested but enthusiastic about the work of the Immaculate. In fact, he allowed Kolbe the services of several monks and three rooms—one as a business office, one for the press operations, and one as a mailing room.

Father Maximilian's cell became the editorial office, and like all editorial offices of any account, it was soon piled everywhere with papers and magazines—on the dressers and stands, under the bed, and even in the middle of the floor.

In the printery, the press had to be turned by hand, from morning till evening, and it took 70,000 revolutions of the big wheel to turn out 5,000 copies of the periodical. If the old torture rack could only have run unattended. But no! There had to be a foot on the treadle and a hand on the wheel.

So whenever Father Maximilian had time free from saying Mass and his Office and hearing confessions, he worked on the press. And at night he did the editorial work in his cell.

Kolbe, please understand, was not what you would call a sophisticated writer. Although he held two degrees, he never flaunted this before the reader. Rather, what made his journalism so effective was the extremely popular style he used. He knew very well that most of his readers were not connoisseurs of great literature, so he took pains to be on their level, to use the same language they did, and to make even complex religious arguments simply understood by the use of dialogue. And then he put into all his writing that fire that was consuming his own soul.

And after every issue that came out, subscriptions always increased. But income still decreased because of the inexorable devaluation of the currency.

One thing that gave both the magazine and the M.I. a big boost was the publishing of some photographs showing the religious of Grodno working in the press room to produce the periodical. This was quite a revelation for some people, who always thought of friars as solitary figures, each almost continually absorbed in his own prayers and very much removed from the everyday labors of ordinary people. Now the camera's lens revealed them as working people in a workers' environment, yet wearing their religious garb and living their consecration to the full.

And to many this seemed like the discovery of a completely new, unheard-of, thoroughly fascinating kind of religious life, because it was so down-to-earth. Several of these wrote in, asking to be admitted to the Order as brothers, "on condition that they could work with Father Maximilian."

Thus a new type of recruit started arriving, and in the religious community a rather delicate situation soon developed for the Polish friaries were at that time still in the process of ridding themselves of some centuries-old traditions which had developed under the feudal system, and one of these was the strict separation between the "fathers" and the "brothers." The latter had traditionally been kept limited in number and had been relegated to the most menial tasks, in a life of total segregation from that of the ordained friars.

This separation had been officially abolished at the turn of the century, but evidently some traces of the old mentality still remained.

Now, however, after the arrival of this first wave of new brothers, and even more so after further waves came rolling in, the ratio of priests to brothers at Grodno changed dramatically. Moreover, the climate created by the M.I. tended to attenuate the age-old distinctions, so that some of these new brothers were given responsibilities formerly held only by the priests.

As might be expected, this caused a certain amount of confusion. Some of the old-timers spoke up in an appeal for more prudence in accepting such "sudden" vocations, and one friar suggested hiring regular employees who would work on the magazine but continue to live in their own homes.

But Father Kolbe replied to this that "only consecrated souls are suitable for the work of the Immaculate." He added that "the work of Mary Immaculate is not a business enterprise," even though it uses the instruments of modern technology. "It is infinitely more than that."

Thus the staff of the *Knight* kept increasing in numbers, and continued joyfully with their work, as, day after day and often into the wee hours of the night, they pushed the treadle with their feet and turned the wheel with their hands. All shared all things equally: the little bread, the abundant hunger, even their clothes, from boots to overalls to overcoats.

Only Father Maximilian's overcoat remained

inviolable, and this because he had to wear it during the day to protect his lungs, and at night he used it to cover himself, for he had given his blanket away to someone else.

6

The Pioneers of Niepokalanów

Auschwitz, August 14, 1941. Bruno Borgowiec watched the hardstepping SS and the groveling Doctor Boch come up the steps of the Bunker, and he knew then that it was all over. With a quick intravenous injection the white-gowned assassin had ended the prolonged martyrdom. The words, "It is finished," came welling up from the recesses of his memory, and an icy sensation gripped his heart.

"The SS guards left, accompanied by the executioner," he wrote a few years later, "and I went back down the stairs, where I found Father Maximilian Kolbe still sitting, propped up against the wall, his eyes wide open and his head inclined to the left, as we were so used to seeing him. His face was radiant with serenity and beauty."

This bit about the radiant face is not something to be attributed to some lyrical excess of Bruno Borgowiec, for his statements are always concise and matter-of-fact. Nor should it be considered a fantasy arising from the unusual emotions of the moment. In a conversation with Father Szweda, who was later collecting material on the life of Father Kolbe, the former secretary-interpreter-undertaker developed his account with detailed precision: "When I opened the iron door, Father Kolbe was no longer alive. His face had an unusual radiance about it. The eyes were wide open and focused on some definite point. His entire person seemed to have been in a state of ecstasy. I will never forget that scene as long as I live."

There was, then, an unusual luminosity radiating from the face of Father Maximilian, there in the shadowy cell, almost as if a veil of brightness had been drawn over his miserably tortured and emaciated members, over his naked and abused body, as if to show the futility of Lagerführer Fritsch's supreme offense against human dignity and of his sacrilegious abomination against the sacredness of a man consecrated to God.

Those wide-open eyes, focused upon some object, the whole person in a state of ecstasy.... Who could resist the thought that in this instant—when he was offering his arm to the fatal needle—the Immaculate, his dear Mamusia, was bringing the reward to her hero, her knight, by appearing once again to him, and leaving in the pupils of his dying eyes a vision of heaven?

But now let us return to a gray dawn sixteen years earlier—the year 1925. At the ancient friary in Grodno the brother who did the cooking arose at his usual early hour and was shuffling half-asleep toward the kitchen, when in the vague first beams of morning strange figures seemed to leap out of the darkness in front of him. The faces were pitch-black. Their hands too, and so were their clothes, and it was impossible to tell what mischief they were intent upon.

It took a few minutes for the poor cook's heart to return to its normal beat, and meanwhile he was wondering if this were still some horrible nightmare or, worse yet, if he were suffering from some sort of hallucination.

But these sinister figures were only fellow friars, as black as chimney sweeps, and covered from tonsure to toe with dust, but still brothers under the skin, God be thanked! These were the friars, lay and ordained, who worked on the printing press and produced the magazine—the personnel of the M.I., up to some of their usual foolishness.

But what had come up during the night to account for this state of affairs that had momentarily threatened the poor cook with a heart attack?

Father Kolbe and his team of coworkers had decided, several months before this incident, to celebrate the Holy Year, 1925, by issuing 12,000 copies of a special 60-page almanac in honor of the Immaculate. It was a senseless sort of undertaking when one considers the prehistoric monster of a press that would have to do the work.

It would have required operating the treadle and turning the wheel for tens of thousands of revolutions, reducing the men who took turns running the press to a state of exhaustion.

Yet in three months, working every day and a good many evenings and giving up all their recreation periods, they did the job.

Judged by any standards of art or business, the most one could say about their almanac was that it had a lot of pages. It was, in fact, such a typographical monstrosity that the publisher felt duty-bound to omit any mention of a price and to apologize profusely to the readers, asking only that they distribute them freely, if they dared, and if they felt in their more generous moments that such a thing might engender in some soul a little bit of love for the Immaculate.

But contrary to all expectations the almanac's success was enormous. The resulting contributions, which came from all over, added up to quite a sum, enabling Father Kolbe to consider for the first time actually replacing his old run-down press with some printing equipment more worthy of the name.

The effect of this sudden financial downpour on Kolbe's imagination was like that of spring rain on fertile ground: ideas for all sorts of new projects began to germinate in his mind. But to one segment of the religious community all this brought was a deep consternation.

Some of the older priests were disturbed about all this money so suddenly acquired and in such abundance, which they considered the responsibility of the whole community. Therefore they did not hesitate to present the guardian, Father Maurice Madzurek, with some words of caution, preoccupied as they were with the risks in which Father Maximilian might involve the whole friary with his "adventurous schemes."

"Let's stop things now, before it's too late. Put the money in safe keeping, maybe in some bank.... All this capital would make a nice little income for the friary.... After all, these are hard times, and the friary needs many repairs, etc., etc."

Father Guardian, enthusiastic as anyone about the work of Mary Immaculate, in his role as a superior could not completely ignore these pleas for prudence on the part of the older fathers. But then something happened that gave an unexpected boost to Father Maximilian's cause.

The provincial, Father Louis Karwacki, paid a visit to Grodno with the special purpose of reviewing the progress made by the magazine. He looked, listened, took notes, and finally gave his blessing to the publishing venture, enrolling himself as a subscriber to the *Knight.* He also gave orders to the guardian to make available to Father Maximilian and his crew a wing of the friary that was presently an uninhabited ruin, as a site for new printing facilities.

But after Father Karwacki left, the opposition reasserted itself and managed to put off any action on the new orders. The delay became almost unbearable for Kolbe and Company.

Then one day, when several of the M.I. printers were working together, one young man got a sudden inspiration. "Why didn't we think of it before? Tell me, didn't Father Provincial give us an order?"

"He certainly did."

"Aren't we duty-bound to obey that order?"

"Of course."

"All right, then. Why are we being so over-scrupulous? Obedience authorizes us to occupy that part of the friary our superior has told us to use for the press."

And that very night brothers and fathers sneaked out of their cells at an hour agreed upon. Ever so quietly they entered what used to be the kitchen and refectory, which was the section of ruins delegated to them, tore down whatever partitions seemed useless to them, dismantled the soot-filled ovens, and before confronting their dissenting fellow friars with the *fait accompli*, unwittingly startled the cook almost out of his mind. That vision of black demons dancing amid the lights and shadows of early dawn was one that the poor brother would not forget to his dying day.

To say they got no scolding or reprimands would be to falsify the record. But what was done, was done, and, recounts the young brother who had conceived the brilliant idea, "We bore it all in a spirit of penitence and humility."

Not long after that, a freight train arrived at the Grodno station, laden with a number of large boxes addressed to the monastery. When these were unpacked inside the spacious quarters of the new print shop, what came to light was a collection of amazing, sparkling new, complicated machines.

They were so complicated, in fact, that when someone playing around with the various knobs and levers finally got the motors started, no one knew how to shut them off. To make matters worse, one of the motors began shooting off loud banging noises like a machine gun, which sent the entire magazine staff scattering.

Just at this very difficult moment a young machinist appeared at the door. "I'd like to become a member of the Militia," he said. But before he had even found out whether his request was to be considered, they almost carried him bodily into the machine-terrorized printery and introduced him to the runaway equipment. With a very experienced air he manipulated a couple of thingamabobs and presto, everything was under control.

From that day on the machines submitted to discipline. To the stepped-up rhythm of the new equipment the periodical staff synchronized their crusade, and the results were phenomenal. "It's all too wonderful," thought Father Maximilian, "and too easy."

But they would pay for their success. It was inevitable. And their ordeal was just around the corner, awaiting them.

The first price was paid by Father Maximilian in his person; he had a relapse of tuberculosis. And at the very time he was being rushed to Zakopane for treatment, Brother Albert Olszakowski, their oldest printer, also helped pay the price. He passed away, more worn out than sick.

"Another has gone to be with the Immaculate. Now we have three collaborators in heaven," was Father Kolbe's quiet comment. His thoughts harked back to Rome, eight years earlier, when the Immaculate had called away Friar Glowinski and Friar Mansi, two charter members of the M.I.

Kolbe's forced absence from the Grodno community, by now the main nerve center of the M.I.'s activities, seemed like a deathblow to the entire work. There were some who felt this very strongly. "It's all over now. Maybe a little flurry of excitement, then everything will be quiet again. Without him, everything will fall apart."

But there was no falling-apart at all, because, in the first place, the M.I. was God's work and Mary Immaculate was in charge of it. Secondly, the "reinforcements in heaven" did not give up their intercession for it. And thirdly the provincial, Father Karwacki, took two precautions at once: first, he transferred Father Alphonse from Cracow to Grodno, and Father Alphonse was actually Joseph Kolbe, Maximilian's brother, and youngest son of Julius Kolbe and Maria Dabrowska. Father Alphonse was put in charge of all his brother's duties for the duration of his absence. Second, he ordered Father Maximilian not to concern himself in any way with either the M.I. or the periodical while he was a patient at Zakopane. Instead, he was to perform "the work of a sick person" and to think only about getting well.

And he obeyed. The order was probably more distressing to him than the sickness itself, but he obeyed just the same, turning a deaf ear to the heart-rending appeals for advice, suggestions, decisions, etc. that came to him from Father Alphonse, who felt utterly disoriented and completely at a loss in the face of his new and very demanding responsibilities.

"Father Provincial has written me not to bother myself about anything there," was big brother's reply, "so I won't be able to give you any counsel or make any of your decisions, because that's what the Immaculate wants. Anything I might do against her will would be a serious mistake. So take care of things in whatever way Mary Immaculate leads you."

Father Alphonse wrote again, made fresh pleas, but always got the same kind of reply. He even made a quick trip to Zakopane, hoping to get guidance of some kind from a face-to-face discussion. But all he got was the same information as before: "I am not supposed to get involved. The Immaculate will help you."

Father Maximilian stuck to his obedience, and by his faithful example helped both the M.I. and his brother onto higher ground. In his letters he tried to help Alphonse see that humble recourse to superiors is a good way to avoid a pack of unnecessary troubles. "Some time ago, the provincial said I could follow the advice of Father Melchior Fordon, and I have profited by this situation ever since, because the Divine Will equals the will of the Immaculate equals the will of Father Provincial equals the advice of Father Fordon."

So Father Alphonse followed his brother's example and the counsels of Father Fordon, and it came to pass that he who had never written an article in his life became a very competent editor. He who had never learned the ABC's of printing raised the circulation of the *Knight* to 60,000 copies. He who had been simply a humble member of the M.I. now became its capable and efficient director.

Then a new wave of affliction broke upon the M.I. Father Fordon seemed about to die from tuberculosis. It was a very unnerved Father Alphonse who wrote once more to his brother to tell him about the impending disaster. Maximilian's reply was simply: "Tell Father Fordon that when he reaches heaven he should not forget the leadership of the M.I., the brothers, the problems we face. And tell him to pray for me too."

Death came to Father Fordon on February 27, 1927. That same April, Father Maximilian was dismissed from Zakopane and returned to Grodno, his soul still bearing the wounds of the ordeal he had gone through during his seven-month illness.

The hardest tribulation had not been the hemorrhages or the other physical sufferings, nor even the rigors of obedience imposed upon him, which had brought him loneliness and taken him away from his very lifework. The supreme test, the trial of trials, had been one that God reserves for those of His children who love Him the most: the dark night of the soul, a time when heaven seems veiled in profound silence and the soul experiences darkness, restlessness, uncertainty, terror, fierce temptations, moral agony. In this moment of abandonment, the light that has been so abundant now disappears from sight, and nothing is visible, nothing understandable, and the soul is no longer able to feel the presence of God.

But even in the very heart of the storm Father Kolbe found a compass of salvation, a beacon that never failed—his immaculate Mamusia. Did he no longer feel her presence, no longer have her before him? "All the better," was his response. "Now I can try to love her with an unselfish love."

When he got back to Grodno, he soon found out that his suffering had borne fruit. In fact, the *Knight* was outgrowing its habitation. Increased space requirements for the presses and other machinery, for paper storage, and for the editorial and administrative offices had resulted in a complete takeover of the friary except for the cells of the friars—and still, this space was becoming more and more inadequate.

The October frosts were just beginning to scatter their chilly whiteness across the endless prairie lands of Prince Drucki Lubecki on the Teresin flats near Warsaw, when the tenant farmers who worked that vast feudal-type estate saw a strange sight. A company of friars had arrived, armed with picks, shovels, hammers, and a modest supply of lumber. They leveled off a piece of land and began to build some rude shacks.

Some months before this, Father Kolbe had heard that the prince, who owned considerable property at Grodno in addition to the vast tract near Warsaw, was interested in disposing of some land in the Teresin area.

Kolbe had gotten in touch with the prince's land agent right away, and then gone to the Grodno station and taken the first train for Warsaw. He had been pleased with what he saw, and had thought to himself that with six acres of this good land he could begin to build the first Niepokalanów or "City of the Immaculate." Here, near Warsaw, he would be in the heart of his native Poland, and just a stone's throw from one of the country's main railroad lines.

"Yes, this has to be the place," he had said. Then, kneeling down, he had opened a bundle he had brought with him, and taken out a little statue of the Immaculate, and planted it among the clods of earth. "My dear Mamusia," he had said, "take possession of this land, for I know it is just what you want."

But when he got back to Grodno and heard what price the prince was asking for the land—and a just price at that—it made his head swim. He told Father Louis Karwacki, his provincial. "If that's the case," said Karwacki, "then I forbid you to buy the land."

Father Maximilian was still using the tried and true equation: the will of the Immaculate equals the will of the provincial. So he went to Prince Drucki Lubecki and told him the deal was off.

"I understand you've put a statue of Our Lady

on that spot," the prince remarked as he was showing Kolbe to the door after the matter appeared closed. "What shall I do with it?"

"You can leave it there," was Kolbe's answer.

There was a moment of silence as the landowner continued to clasp the friar's hand. "Very well, then. The land goes with the statue. I make you a present of it."

"Kneel, my children, and give thanks to Mary Immaculate," were Father Maximilian's first words to his co-workers when he got back to the printery at the Friary. And three resounding "Hail Marys" rose above the rumble of the machinery as an expression of everyone's heartfelt gratitude.

The prince's tenants, many of them Jewish, very thoughtfully looked after the nutritional needs of these friar-carpenters by bringing them some baskets of food, since the friars, intent as they were on procuring tools and materials, had all but forgotten that they would need to eat.

Father Kolbe worked alongside the other friars and shared their hardships, arising with them before dawn and traveling to and from Warsaw to fetch needed supplies. And all this time he was carrying in his wallet some medical instructions given him by the physician in Zakopane: "A life of relaxation and regularity, plenty of food and sleep, several hours of rest in a deck chair, and positively no lifting or carrying."

On November 21, 1927, the prince's tenants realized they would have to enlarge their hearts and increase the number of food baskets, because on that day the advance unit was joined by the remainder of the M.I. staff. Now that the new "friary" was built, everyone had left Grodno in order to give a hand to constructing a shelter for the press equipment.

A raw recruit for the M.I. arrived one day, without having been briefed on the "Kolbe technique" beforehand. "Excuse me," he asked one of the peasants, "can you tell me how to reach the Niepokalanów friary? I've been looking all over the place, and haven't seen anything that looks like a friary."

"Over there!" the farmer replied, pointing with his big, calloused hand to some wooden shacks nearby.

"That's the *friary*?" the poor rookie gasped.

"That's it, all right! That's *our* Niepokalanów.... Look here, son, don't get scared till you look it over close up, 'cause those fellows over there are really happy. I'm telling you! You should hear them—always singing."

Father Maximilian also noticed the youth's bewilderment when he showed up a few minutes later. "Come, my boy; you must be quite tired and hungry. You will be happy here, my son, if you will love the Immaculate and seek to belong to her always. Very happy!"

One of the builders of Niepokalanów wrote later: "I actually believe that no father or mother ever loved their children with as much affection and tenderness as Father Maximilian loved us."

And another later said, "Whenever I was near him, I felt like a child in the arms of its mother."

The succeeding years passed quickly, and with each new year Niepokalanów increased in numbers and in activity, and each year new buildings sprang up to accommodate the increase.

After ten years in the center of Niepokalanów a vast H-shaped publishing complex had arisen, consisting of editorial offices, a library, type storage, a linotype department, an engraving plant, photographic darkrooms, a press room, a central engine room complete with electrical substation, a bindery, the shipping department, and a warehouse.

Alongside this main group of buildings was another, centered around the chapel: the general administrative offices, the postulants' living quarters, the novitiate, the friars' dormitories, the huge refectory (where everybody, absolutely everybody, ate from a tin plate and drank from a tin cup), the electric power station, a small infirmary, a first aid station, and a dentist's office. In various other locations scattered throughout the city were the workshops for the carpenters, shoemakers, tailors, metal workers, and mechanics, as well as a brickyard, a railway line linked to the national rail system, a parking lot, and a fire station.

In the early days of Niepokalanów, the wooden buildings made the danger of sudden fires a very serious problem. On five different occasions, in fact, the city was threatened with complete destruction, and each time the cry went up: "Make

way! Here come the Knights of the Immaculate!"
And sure enough, there were the fireman-friars, in
their helmets and gas masks, dressed and equipped
in short order, arriving with their fire truck, ready
to save the day.

"I simply can't understand it!" commented
one visiting religious during a tour of the place.
"Here technology and mysticism go hand in hand."

Then there was the businessman who came
hoping to get a few orders. "I'm a Communist," he
told them confidentially, "but I'll have to admit that
this is the first time I ever saw my ideas actually put
into practice. Why, you're the *real* communists!"

But in 1930, in the midst of all these
developments, Father Maximilian Kolbe had taken
a leave of absence from Niepokalanów because he
felt the call of the Immaculate. She was asking him
to journey halfway around the world and to found
another "City of the Immaculate" in the land of the
cherry blossoms.

7

From Nagasaki to Auschwitz

The train puffed and groaned as it labored monotonously on its way, waving a slender pennant of white smoke above its head. The endless green plains, stretching out to the blue horizon in every direction, seemed to be absent-mindedly repeating themselves hour after hour. Inside the careening passenger cars the old wooden seats screeched out the ballad of their woes to the rhythmic accompaniment of the metallic click-clacks from the racing wheels.

At Warsaw a friar boarded. Then some Japanese youths. "Must be exchange students," thought the friar when he spied them. His assumption was soon confirmed when, by pooling their vocabulary of several living and one or two "dead" languages, he and they were able to piece together a kind of conversation.

This international dialogue became ever more

cordial as the hours wore on. By the time it became necessary to say reluctant goodbyes to one another, they were like old friends parting. The friar's last gesture was to reach within the cavernous folds of his Franciscan habit and pull out a handful of Miraculous Medals, offering one to each student as a memoir of their happy time together. Deeply touched, they countered his gift with some little wooden fetishes bearing the likeness of elephants.

Time and again, during the months that followed this encounter, Father Maximilian took these strange little idols in his hands, and each time he was deeply pained at the thought of those dear brethren so far away who were ignorant of the God and Father of us all and of the House that He has prepared for us to live in.

Out of this suffering grew a plan, which gradually matured, until one day toward the end of 1929, when Niepokalanów was barely two years old, he laid his proposal before the new provincial, Father Czupryk, concluding his remarks with a very simple statement: "So now I have come asking permission to go to Japan and found there another City of the Immaculate."

If Father Czupryk was not yet convinced of the "madness" involved in such a proposal, he certainly must have been after hearing Kolbe's answers to the three questions that he immediately fired back: "What sort of financial support do you have?"

"Not a penny."

"Do you know any Japanese?"

"Not a word."

"But do you have at least one friend over there that you could count on to help you out?"

"Not yet, but by God's grace I hope to find one."

During the embarrassing silence that followed, there was more to be discerned from the superior's troubled face than his words could ever have expressed. This Kolbe fellow, it was true, had already proved at Niepokalanów, and earlier at Grodno, that he was one of those rare individuals who could harvest crops from the desert and make something significant out of what was originally nothing. But up till now all of Kolbe's accomplishments had been confined to the Polish milieu. He had worked entirely among his own people and in a culture where Catholicism was taken for granted. He had never been out to the ends of the earth, or dwelt among an utterly alien people who had no knowledge of the one God, or who had too many other gods. One must be prudent. Yes, that was it, prudence!

Father Maximilian got the message, and he knew that once again he must entrust himself to the will of God and to his immaculate Mamusia. Meanwhile he would do his part, which he did by begging Father Czupryk to approve his project, even if it *did* sound crazy—or at least to consider it as a possibility! He even wrote out his proposal, so that it could be reread at Father Provincial's convenience and shared with his fellow superiors.

But almost in the same breath, and with the same energy and enthusiasm, he urged his provincial not to let himself be unduly influenced by either his spoken or his written words, but to make his decision with complete freedom and the exercise of good judgment. "I wish to do only one thing, and that is to obey blindly, for I am confident that the Immaculate will manifest her wishes through my superiors."

Scarcely three weeks later Kolbe was in Rome to receive official permission from the Franciscan Minister General for the new work he was about to begin. On his way back to Niepokalanów he went to Lourdes to seek the blessing of the Immaculate. "Here," he wrote, "you can feel the Immaculate's presence." Then he went to Lisieux to ask the help of St. Therese. "I saw here the chessmen used by St.' Therese. Let this be a consolation to all our unrepentent chess players!"

On February 26, 1930, a group of friars gathered at the Warsaw station to bid farewell to several of their number who were setting off for the missions. As the train pulled out they waved their handkerchiefs, and from his window Father Maximilian responded, energetically waving his arms until those left behind were out of sight. With him on this new adventure were four of the younger religious brothers. Their first destination was Rome, then on to Marseilles, France, where they would embark for the Far East on March 7. "Operation Japan" had begun.

Throughout the seven-week voyage Kolbe and his fellow friars camped out on the ship's deck with the poorest class of passengers, sharing all their inconveniences and discomforts.

Father Maximilian put himself at their service, preaching much more by his example than by word of mouth. During his few leisure moments he began to tackle the complexities of the Japanese language.

It was April 24, 1930, when Nagasaki finally loomed on the horizon, vast and captivating. The ship headed for the port city, slipping past picturesque little islets decked out with cherry blossoms and bamboo cottages.

"A pleasant surprise awaits you in more than one of those little huts, Father," a fellow passenger remarked to Kolbe as they stood on deck, watching the islands coast by. "Every home, of course, has its shrine honoring the forces of nature, the ancestors, the ancient heroes of Shintoism, and various Buddhist gods and goddesses. But the big surprise is to find in some of these pantheons a little statue of Our Lady. They call her "Seibo," but she is actually the Blessed Mother, even if you can hardly distinguish her from the goddess Kwanom. These statues are the last tell-tale traces of an early Christian movement in Japan. Christianity flourished here three centuries ago, and then was suppressed—in a blood bath, as you probably know...."

"But I wonder how many Christians today in the West know that or ever think of it," Kolbe replied, gazing thoughtfully at the Hill of Martyrs, a slate-blue silhouette in the creamy sky above Nagasaki.

On that mountain many thousands of Japanese (the exact number unknown) were tortured and massacred three hundred years ago, faithful to their last breath to that message of love brought them by a few missionaries from the faraway West. He recalled that among these forgotten martyrs was one of his own countrymen, Adalbert Mecinski, who had come to Japan with a most ardent desire to be a martyr for his faith. Then, looking up to heaven, he prayed quietly: "Mamusia, my Mamusia, is it here you have planned to give me that lovely red crown?"

His Excellency Bishop Hayasaki, the local ordinary, couldn't help smiling indulgently while Father Kolbe, who had descended on the episcopal residence in Nagasaki as soon as the boat was docked, spoke to him enthusiastically of his plans to publish a Japanese-language periodical. This Pole had landed in Japan just a few hours ago, knowing nothing about the Japanese people, their language, their customs or moral standards, their national characteristics or emotional makeup—and to top it all off, he didn't have a penny in his pocket.

The prelate's smile broadened when, with candid simplicity, the unpredictable Franciscan proceeded to present him with nothing less than a plan he had for founding a "city." Nevertheless, the bishop heard him out without comment. Then he sorted out, from that sea of good intentions, the one idea that seemed to have any concrete application. "So, Father," he replied at last, "you have mentioned to me that you have doctorates in theology and philosophy. Very good, and would you have any reluctance to teaching some courses here in my seminary?"

"Oh, on the contrary, I would be glad to do so. But on one condition: that Your Excellency allow me to publish my periodical for the Immaculate."

Every trace of the smile vanished from the good bishop's face. So the friar wasn't giving in! A determined sort of fellow, apparently. In those kind but firm eyes he seemed to see something truly profound. "Very well, then," he said, "we will not deny Our Lord any opportunity." He moved his hand in a blessing, and the big pastoral ring seemed to sparkle a little more than usual.

On May 24, 1930, exactly a month after Father Maximilian Kolbe landed at Nagasaki, a telegram arrived at Niepokalanów, MAILING FIRST ISSUE STOP HAVE PRINTSHOP STOP VIVA IM-MACULATA STOP MAXIMILIAN.

Incredible as his success had been, it was far from magical, in spite of someone's joking sug-gestion to the contrary. Father Maximilian's whole program could be reduced to a simple formula composed of only two ingredients, but each of them in generous doses: first, much prayer; second, strict poverty. The prayer brought response from heav-en; the poverty brought a response from men.

This is because the Japanese are lovers of heroism, and the kind of heroism they prize most highly is that of total dedication of self to a good cause. The Japanese judge a stranger by the measure of his own ideals, and their admiration for him increases in proportion to the hardships he is willing to undergo to be consistent with the ideals he professes. Thus it becomes clear that Father Kolbe and his little band of helpers possessed, from the very first day, all the necessary credentials for securing the people's respect and admiration.

They lived in a run-down house (which he referred to as "Grodno") whose roof was badly in need of repair: "Last night we had a real snowstorm. The snow came right in on us, and this morning the inside of our dormitory was white."

They ate just what was needed to keep alive, using Japanese recipes, usually unappetizing to a European, and especially so to Father Maximilian. They had to prepare their meals outdoors, and on rainy days this made the food rather soggy. But they never asked anyone for anything, outside of inviting the Japanese they met to be partakers of their own happiness.

Thus it happened that in a very short time he had enlisted a group of enthusiastic collaborators and accumulated a sum big enough to buy such a granddaddy of a printing press that it made the old-timer he had used in 1922 at Grodno seem modern by comparison. "It's as rusty as it can be and won't run unless we use all our strength on it. So after we get through wrestling with it, our hands are all bloody.

But even more fatiguing than the presswork for *Mugenzai no Seibo no Kishi* (Japanese for "Knight of the Immaculate") was the problem of

121

typesetting in Japanese. The poor friars could not make heads or tails of those thousands of bewildering characters.

As for editing the articles, this was an adventure of its own. Father Kolbe was once again the only editor, doing his mental work after hours, when he could be spared the more back-breaking labor. He wrote the articles in Latin, after which they were translated into Japanese by a young Japanese Methodist, who had been inspired by the heroism of the friars to join them in their cause. He persisted in helping them, and eventually decided to become a Catholic and a member of the M.I.

Ten thousand copies of the first issue were printed. The work of distribution was handled by a team of volunteer "newsboys" who went about the city soliciting subscriptions, and whose technique was carefully designed to comply with the exacting demands of Oriental courtesy.

Try to imagine this scene, repeated thousands of times in the streets of Nagasaki and on the roads leading out of town. The salesman spies a man whom he feels is a good prospect for a subscription. He comes up to him, bowing and smiling, and with the utmost courtesy offers him a copy of the paper, requesting in return only the gentleman's calling card. If the prospect accepts this offer and with a polite little bow and equally polite smile hands over his card, then the solicitation of his subscription can proceed.

This little ritual was absolutely necessary

because never, under any circumstances, would the exquisite finesse of Japanese manners have tolerated someone's violent intrusion into the affairs of another (which is what sending a copy to the person's home would have been considered) without the addressee having given the sender some token of his consent, symbolized in this case by his presenting him with a calling card.

Even allowing for the effectiveness of this attention to the complex details of Nipponese etiquette, the immediate acceptance of *Mugenzai no Seibo no Kishi* exceeded even the wildest dreams of Father Kolbe, which is saying quite a bit. Many Japanese, especially the intellectuals, were at that time experiencing a spiritual void, having abandoned the traditional Japanese religious practices in favor of a sort of blind atheistic cult of nationalism. Crying out amid this spiritual emptiness there was now the modest voice of a simple little review that spoke out plainly, compellingly, radically. But what meant most to its readers was something that almost leaped out of every printed line—the fact that it was the genuine expression of the heroic life lived by a handful of men united in their dedication to a great ideal.

But as the work of the Immaculate gained in favor from week to week, Father Maximilian's health grew poorer day by day. He was plagued by a recurrent fever and violent migraines; and insomnia prevented him from finding relief even at night. His body became covered with abscesses to the point where he could hardly walk. For a time he had to celebrate Mass standing on one foot, sometimes finding it necessary to have an assistant support him by the arms.

But despite all this he kept steadily on course. "When our work has really taken root here in Japan, then I want to go to India, and afterwards to the Arabs in Beirut. I plan to publish the periodical in Turkish, Persian, Arabic, and Hebrew. A billion readers! Half the world's people!"

Instead, he was obliged to return to Poland. He had been but a few months in Japan when instructions came to present himself before the provincial chapter, which was to meet in Lwów at the earliest possible date.

Thus he had to leave at a very critical moment in the development of his work, with no one to whom he could really entrust its management—no one he could rely on to keep the movement alive, let alone promote its expansion. To Kolbe it was an experience comparable only to that of a mother called upon to abandon her offspring at a moment when for its survival her presence is critically needed, indeed indispensable. He left with a bleeding heart.

He reached Lwów in very poor condition, after an overland trip through the vast, endless reaches of the Soviet Union, huddled together with an uncomfortable crowd of soldiers, laborers, and peasants in a densely packed compartment of the Trans-Siberian Railway.

The meeting of the provincial chapter came to order, with an important item of business on the agenda: Kolbe and his "Operation Japan." Chief objection: the whole adventure was utterly foolhardy. Proposed solution: withdraw at once, before things went too far.

Father Maximilian Kolbe took the floor, and said his say, after which he bowed his head, closed his eyes, and hid his hands in the sleeves of his habit. Inside one sleeve of a friar's habit was a little pocket where the wearer kept his watch, if he happened to own one. Father Kolbe used it for his rosary, and this he began to finger, saying one "Hail Mary" after another, while his superiors discussed the fate of his "foolhardy adventure."

"I've done all I could," he murmured after completing the "Hail Holy Queen." "Now, Mamusia, it's up to you."

Only after this did he pay any attention to the discussion going on around him, only to discover that "Operation Japan" had been approved. Not only would he be sent back, but with more authority than before.

When he got back to Nagasaki, he found everything at a standstill. All work had ceased. The press itself was rustier and stiffer than ever. Everything gave the impression that *Mugenzai no Seibo no Kishi* would make no further appearances. It seemed that there were only two alternatives: give up, or start all over again. Naturally, Maximilian Kolbe wasted no time getting to work.

A year later, and a miracle seemed to have taken place. Close your eyes and imagine the scene with me. Instead of the six acres of the Teresin steppe near Warsaw, imagine another six acres, purchased for 7,000 yen, on the slopes of Hikosan, the mountain that dominates Nagasaki and its outlying islands. Instead of the infinitely flat steppes of central Poland, picture for yourself cherry orchards climbing skyward up the hill. Instead of the tall, blond brothers of Niepokalanów, imagine short-legged, black-haired friars with almond-shaped eyes—and then you will have a picture of Mugenzai no Sono, the "Garden of the Immaculate," as it appeared in 1931. There is a tile-roofed wooden building thirty feet wide and seventy-five feet long, divided into a large working area and a smaller living area, which includes a tiny chapel.

If you invest this little "Garden of the Immaculate," with the same vitality and capacity for growth that characterized Niepokalanów, then you have a good idea what sort of development the M.I. was to experience in Nagasaki and other Japanese cities.

Already in 1931 the magazine was the most widely distributed Catholic periodical then printed in a non-Christian country. It was proving to be a repetition of the Polish miracle. Its sphere of influence grew to the point where groups of Buddhist monks would come and spend many hours conversing with Father Maximilian about the truths of his faith. "From now on," one Buddhist monk declared as he emerged from one such encounter, "I'm not going to admit anyone into my monastery who does not love our *Seibo no Kishi,* the Immaculate."

The period 1930–31 had been a time of incredible activity, and the burden of much of it had fallen on Father Kolbe's shoulders. Moreover, he and his fellow friars had undergone tremendous sacrifices, experienced moments of bitter sorrow, and lived on an impossible diet. And all of this, combined with a longing for their faraway home-land, had even caused some of the friars to leave him and return to Poland. "However," he wrote, "for each one who flees in discouragement, two more advance to the front," so that in addition to the small group of Polish brothers, he now had an increasing number of Japanese in his community.

There were those who criticized him for his choice of location. "What an out-of-the-way place. A charming site, no doubt about it, but very inconvenient—on the slope of a mountain and too far from the business district of Nagasaki."

Kolbe would just shrug his shoulders and smile at his critics. Not too many years would pass before the importance of his choice was to be demonstrated. When the atomic apocalypse was unleashed on Nagasaki, the entire city was blown off the face of the map, but over on the slopes of Hikosan, Mugenzai no Sono was scarcely damaged at all: just a few broken windowpanes, and none of the inhabitants injured in any way.

In May 1936, Maximilian Kolbe returned to Poland to take part in the Provincial Chapter in Cracow. Despite his poor health, the Chapter appointed him guardian of Niepokalanów, whose population had increased by now to include more than 500 professed religious and nearly 200 aspirants to the religious life. It had truly become, as one friar put it, "a republic of consecrated working people," where everyone, from the priest-editor to the brother who served as printer's devil, wore the same work-worn habits, and all lived in the same spirit of brotherhood that had characterized the city's beginnings.

Already in 1936, dark thunderclouds could be seen rising out of Berlin and reaching out to threaten all of Europe's skies. Fully aware of this, Father Kolbe occupied himself only with living the present moment for the glory of God, which meant taking a new and breathtaking spurt forward in his creative activities.

His first step was to draw up a comprehensive organizational plan for the "city," which would safeguard and promote the spiritual life and physical well-being of the friars, while maximizing the efficiency and effectiveness of Niepokalanów's phenomenal editorial and publishing activities. This new organization went into effect December 8, 1936.

During the following years, Niepokalanów's publishing operations continued to expand and diversify, reaching out to ever-greater numbers of people. By the end of 1938, the *Knight of the Immaculate,* the monthly that had been Niepokalanów's pioneer publication, had a circulation of 800,000 and had given birth to some very healthy children: the *Young Knight of the Immaculate,* an illustrated monthly for youth, selling 170,000 copies, and the *Little Knight of the Immaculate,* an illustrated monthly for children, selling 30,000 copies. That same year Kolbe began to publish *Miles Immaculatae,* a Latin quarterly for priests and religious of other countries, whose circulation quickly climbed to 15,000. Two other monthlies were also published by Niepokalanów: the *Militia Bulletin,* a publication for the Marian focus groups, and the *Mission Bulletin,* born of Kolbe's continued concern for his "beloved pagans." Niepokalanów also had its own weekly newsletter for the inhabitants of the "city": the *Echo of Niepokalanów.*

But by far the most impressive branch on this great "tree" which had grown out of the *Knight,* that first little "seed" planted and nurtured with the gifts of the poor, was something very dear to the heart of the Polish bishops, a dream that had come true at last: a Catholic daily paper, *Maly Dyiennik (The Little Journal).* Well edited and aggressive, it gave a clear sense of direction to the Catholic masses, above and beyond the viewpoints of the various political parties and special interest groups. Moreover it was priced below any other daily. *The Little Journal* had met with immediate success, and by 1939 it was selling 135,000 copies daily and 225,000 on Sundays, in eleven regional editions.

On December 8, 1938, Niepokalanów's own radio transmitter went into operation, and soon afterward Kolbe began taking preliminary steps to sign up the better Polish actors, with a view toward beginning full-scale production of Christian films. He was also planning the construction of an airport, first link in a transportation chain that would connect future "cities of the Immaculate" in the various countries.

Then came September 1939, when death rained suddenly from the skies, and in its wake the Nazi Attila brought in his steel-helmeted Huns, trampling every form of resistance and leaving only ashes behind.

As the Nazis Wermacht relentlessly advanced across Poland, the Polish government ordered the evacuation of Niepokalanów. Father Kolbe there-upon sent each friar off to his own family, and only he and some thirty-five of those who had been with him from the very beginning remained.

On September 19, the Nazi troops descended on Niepokalanów. Its few remaining inhabitants were ordered to line up, and were then led off and made to climb unceremoniously into waiting cattle cars, their final destination: Amtitz Concentration Camp.

A book could be written just on Kolbe's activities in this camp. Here we will mention only one episode passed on to us by a fellow prisoner named Juraszek: "One night, startled out of sleep, I discovered myself being covered very gently with a blanket. It was Father. Every time I am reminded of him, I can't help crying. I remember seeing him slip part of his food ration to a brother who was suffering more from the food shortage than some of the others. And the ration was so small to begin with that only a mother's heart could have been moved to reduce its size any further."

On the feast of the Immaculate Conception, they were unexpectedly released. Father Kolbe headed at once for Niepokalanów, which he found in a ransacked condition. In the days that followed, one after another of his friars returned from various sections of their convulsed country.

"Let us pray," he told them, "let us lovingly accept all our crosses, and let us love every neighbor, whether friend or enemy, without distinction." At this time he inaugurated the practice of perpetual adoration at Niepokalanów.

Then, on February 17, 1941, a young brother darted excitedly into his room. "Father," he gasped, all out of breath, "they've come...a black car... it's...the Gestapo." Then other brothers came running in.

"Very well then, my sons," Kolbe told them, "I'm on my way. The Immaculate..." but he didn't finish the sentence. Perhaps he meant: "She is calling me. She is about to give me the red crown she promised."

He looked thin, frail, almost transparent as he moved toward the five big Germans waiting outside. "Praised be Jesus Christ!" he greeted them.

"Are you Father Maximilian Kolbe?"

"Yes, I am."

"Come with us!" The black limousine seemed more like a hearse. Father Kolbe looked back just

131

once more, before they took him away, his eyes embracing and caressing his city and his children for the last time. "And now, Mamusia, I must go, and you will have to take my place," he said. "Be the guardian of your little domain—all its sheep and lambs—even the poor goats. I turn everything over to you."

Then they shoved him roughly inside, closed the door with a loud slam, and took him to the earthly inferno known as Pawiak. One little story will give you an idea of the sufferings Kolbe underwent in this infamous prison.

One day an official of the SS, the *Schaarführer*, made a tour of inspection among the prisoners. On opening cell 13 and seeing a friar's habit, he literally went mad with rage. He leaped upon Father Kolbe like some beast of prey, seized the large rosary hanging around his waist, tore it off, and held the wooden crucifix under his nose: "Imbecile! Idiot! Filthy pig of a priest! Do you believe in this stuff?"

"Most certainly I believe!"

He struck Father Kolbe a blow on the left cheek, then another on the right. Blood started trickling from Kolbe's mouth. "Do you still believe?"

"Yes, I believe as much as ever."

Another volley of blows rained down upon him, accompanied by some horrible blasphemy. "And now will you tell me you still believe?"

"Yes, just as much as ever."

Then the *Schaarführer*, a big six-footer flew at

Kolbe, striking him again and again until he fell to the ground in agony.

But after the tormentor had left, slamming the door shut amid the boisterous laughs of his fellow SS men, and Kolbe's weeping cellmates clustered around him, they heard him whisper, "This is no time to weep, my friends, but to rejoice. All this is for the good of souls, for Mary Immaculate...."

As a result of the beating he had received, Kolbe came down with pneumonia and was admitted to a sort of makeshift infirmary. In the days that followed, twenty of his fellow friars offered themselves as hostages in exchange for his release. The Gestapo gave but one answer to these generous offers: as soon as Kolbe was ambulatory, he and a crowd of other unfortunates were herded onto a cattle car for what was to be his last earthly journey—to Auschwitz.

We have already noted what happened in this camp and in the Starvation Bunker between the end of July and August 14, 1941: the escape of a prisoner from Block 14...collective punishment under the blistering sun...the sadistic choice of ten special victims...Sergeant Gajowniczek's uncontrollable grief over his wife and children, still living...the incredible act of love that was like a burst of radiant light in that dreadful night of human hatred, when one man offered to die for another, "the one who has a wife and children"...the descent into the Bunker—"My Lady, my Queen, my Mother, my Mamusia, you have kept

133

your word; for this moment I was born"...the beautiful deep red sunset out there, beyond the barbed wire....

But in addition to these last days in the Bunker, much light has also been shed on the events of the preceding period, from April to July 1941. A patient search for the surviving witnesses has made this possible. And their sworn testimony points to only one conclusion: the sacrifice Kolbe made of his life for the life of another was not the result of sudden, blind compassion, nor an impetuous flash of heroism that burst forth at a highly dramatic moment, but the final gesture of an unbounded love that had to, almost logically at this point, crown a crescendo of self-giving gestures with the total and supreme offering. To use the striking words of a fellow prisoner, "After all the acts of love he performed in the barbed wire enclosure of Auschwitz, I'd have been more surprised if he hadn't made the supreme sacrifice than I am by the fact that he did...."

It should be enough to cite a few passages, taken here and there from some of the many existing testimonies—beginning with the very man whose life was saved by Kolbe—to verify this conclusion.

"I spoke with him for the first time one day in the middle of June, 1941," says ex-Sergeant Francis Gajowniczek, today a city employee at Brzeg on the Oder. "We were working together in a task force assigned to farm work, pitching manure out of a ditch. We made the usual small talk—Where are you from? What did you do before? He counseled me to pray and to place myself in Mary's care. He insisted that only through prayer and the help of the Immaculate would I persevere to the end. I had already taken notice of him some time before this, during the nights in Block 14. Not only would he kneel in fervent prayer, something strictly forbidden, but he would edge over to where his companions were lying and secretly hear their confessions. This was punishable by death. He also led groups in prayer and even went so far as to give conferences. One Sunday I myself attended one of these clandestine meetings. It was held just outside of our block. He spoke about Our Lady.... His love for those around him was extraordinary. He looked after everyone, and in particular the 'Moslems.' In camp jargon the word 'Moslem' was used to describe the prisoners who were almost completely worn away, reduced to skin and bone, for all practical purposes, already dead. The most splendid confirmation of his heroic love for his fellow men was to come at the end, when he offered his life for none other than me, almost a total stranger to him.... For himself, instead, he sought nothing, not even food or clothing. He was content with what little was given him and even this he shared with the others. Not even when he was assigned to peel potatoes did he try to pilfer a few extra morsels from the large kettles—as all the others did—nor would he so much as gather up the scraps to help him survive.... He underwent hardships and beatings with unbelievable calm, never disheartened, never uttering the slightest criticism.

"I remember one day when we were working with the manure, a member of the SS hit him savagely in the face several times and then ordered his dog to attack. The dog went at him repeatedly, biting him and tormenting him. Father Kolbe bore all this with dignified patience, and then he climbed back down into the ditch and we continued to pitch out the manure. He had not complained once as he was being struck, and even afterwards he did not utter a single word against that savage guard."

Instead Father Kolbe prayed for his oppressors and urged his fellow prisoners in Block 14 to do the same, to implore God for the salvation of their souls. One of several confirmations of this comes from the words of Henry Alexander Sienkiewicz, now a Polish forest ranger.

"Father Kolbe had been assigned to work for a few days with a detachment of priests and Jews," recounts Sienkiewicz. "They were constructing a new crematorium. His job was to haul gravel, but in an oversized wheelbarrow with a wheel disproportionately undersized. The strain on him was crushing. I couldn't bring myself to let him go it alone, so I stopped him and offered to make a few trips in his place. At that moment, the guard noticed us talking together in low voices. He stormed down on us and began beating the both of us. Then, to make us look ridiculous before the others, he ordered Father Kolbe to take up the loaded wheelbarrow again, with me now sitting on top, push it to where it was to be unloaded, return with me in the emptied wheelbarrow for a new load, get on top of it himself and have me haul him back and forth. We alternated for a few times like this. It took super-human effort considering the condition we were reduced to. 'Don't lose heart, Henry,' he encouraged me. 'Everything that we suffer is for the Immaculate. Even in something like this, we have to be for them—he nodded toward the Nazis—confessors of Mary. . . . '"

Shortly after this, Sienkiewicz was assigned to a detachment that left the camp every day to work at Bunawerke together with some non-prison workers.

"I managed to gain the trust of these civilian workers—his testimony reads—and every so often they would slip me some bread, a little money, and a few other articles. One day I was able to get past the Camp guards with 400 marks and thirty medals, all of which I handed over to Father Maximilian. He divided up the money among the prisoners of Block 14 along with the medals, after he had blessed them. I could have gotten food too, but it would have been too risky trying to bring it into camp because we were carefully searched at the entrance gate. Nevertheless I asked Father Kolbe's advice on the matter. He said to me, 'Place yourself under the protection of Mary Immaculate; I will pray and she will help you.' This was how I began bringing food into the Camp. And things went smoothly, so much so that one evening I decided to risk bringing a 4-pound round-loaf, which I hid under my coat, and two 2-pound cakes of lard, secured under the wrappings around the calves of each of my legs. At the gate I was scrupulously searched by an SS guard. My heart was in my throat. Finally he nodded for

137

me to pass. He hadn't discovered a thing. 'Trust always in the Immaculate—Father Kolbe again told me—and she will yet shed her favors on you more than a few times.'"

One day, Henry Sienkiewicz returned to Block 14 with a little container. Father Kolbe opened it. Inside there were a small number of hosts. They had been prepared by a good woman named Kania. With the greatest of secrecy, Father Kolbe managed to celebrate two Masses, at each of which some thirty prisoners took part. They all received Communion.

In June of 1941, Maximilian Kolbe was assigned to the "Babice" detachment, commanded by the infamous Krott and responsible for the most grueling labor at Auschwitz—cutting reeds along the river Sola.

"All of us in that detachment—recounts Dr. Ladislaus Lewkowicz, a veterinarian of Poznan—sought out every possible way to avoid at least the more exhausting work. But not Kolbe. 'It's all the same to me,' he would say, 'I only desire that God's will be done.' Yet, in spite of Kolbe's willingness to work, one day Krott began to beat him ruthlessly. But not even this would draw a bitter word from his lips. To the contrary. He said he was happy to suffer 'because everything comes from the Lord.'"

As a result of this beating, he was forced to enter the hospital for a while. Because of its limited space the Camp hospital was for the prisoners the least available of all possible refuges. Yet previous to this, Father Kolbe had had several opportunities to be admitted. He had declined each time. The documentation of this fact is taken from what I consider to be the most important testimony that has come to us from the survivors of Auschwitz: that of Rudolf Diem, a Polish physician of the Evangelical faith. He was assigned to the hospital at the Auschwitz extermination camp for four years.

"He was burning with fever when he arrived at Auschwitz," recalls Dr. Diem, "and suffering from chest pains. But he was serene. At times, he would get in the long line with those prisoners who wished to be examined by a doctor. These were usually lines of 400 to 500 persons, and sometimes even a thousand. Yet he would patiently await his turn, and, if it came up, he would ask for medical advice and some medicine. He was serene, completely in control, psychologically sound in every way. He immediately attracted my attention because from the very first visit, he refused to heed my warning that the gravity of his illness required his hospitalization. He said that he could wait awhile longer and suggested that I give the available post to some other prisoner whom he then indicated to me...."

Here is indisputable testimony, by a Protestant doctor, that Father Kolbe's sacrifice had begun long before he offered his life to save the father of a family.

"And that wasn't the only time he declined to enter the hospital," continues Dr. Diem. "He did so repeatedly on following occasions. Though he urgently needed hospital care, he would always point out other prisoners who, as he saw it, were in greater need. Confounded by this kind of behavior, so inconceivable in that inferno, I finally had to ask him who he was. A Catholic priest,' he answered. Which prompted me to ask him if he still managed to believe that God was watching over us. Believe he did, and he tried with all his effort to convince me also. In fact, he proposed that we meet together during our free time to speak more at length. I went a few times, and it was precisely about questions of faith that we talked. I kept insisting that in that climate of moral deprivation and horrendous mass crimes, I found it absolutely impossible to continue believing in the existence of God. And with never the slightest gesture of hatred toward the invaders responsible for so many atrocities, he would assure me that one day I would again believe. Perhaps because he wanted to be of the greatest possible help to me, he offered to hear my confession. It was then that I told him I was Protestant. But this made no difference: 'Doctor,' he continued, 'you have done so much for me that I would like to repay you in some way.' He then invited me to speak with him again on future occasions....

"I wasn't present in the quadrangle when the Lagerführer Fritsch selected the ten who were to die in the Bunker, but immediately afterwards I received word of what had happened from the many prisoners who came to me for medical aid. They did not begin to understand the greatness of

140

that sacrifice. I did. In that concentration camp where the overall struggle for life, set in motion in each one there by the survival instinct, was at the bottom of every thought and every action of every prisoner, Father Kolbe, with his moral outlook, that is, with his living faith in the Lord and in Providence, with his Christian hope, and above all with his love for God and neighbor, was already far beyond the comprehension of all the others, and well distinguished from them even before his final heroic gesture. I can say with certainty that I never knew a man like him at Auschwitz, though every day I dealt with hundreds upon hundreds of prisoners—priests, religious, professors, noblemen, artists, men from every social strata and walk of life. I'd like to emphasize: I was attached to that Camp from January of 1941 to January of 1945 and I never saw such a sublime example of love of neighbor...."

On Friday, August 15, the feast of the Assumption, twenty-four hours after Father Maximilian Kolbe's life had been "scientifically" terminated, Bruno Borgowiec and another prisoner, who served as the barber for the SS, came to remove his body from the washroom where they had placed it the day before. They put it in a rough wooden box and then carried it to the incinerator to be cremated.

Thus, of all the millions of human beings who lost their lives at Auschwitz, Father Maximilian

Kolbe was possibly the only one to be honored with a coffin for his remains and something resembling funeral rites.

Here in a few rapid strokes of the brush is the story of a man who once told his brethren, in a meeting at Niepokalanów, "I insist that you become saints, and great saints! Does that surprise you? But remember, my children, that holiness is not a luxury, but a simple duty. It is Jesus who told us to be perfect as our Father in heaven is perfect. So do not think it is such a difficult thing. Actually, it is a very simple mathematical problem. Let me show you on the blackboard my formula for sanctity. Then you will see how simple it is. Do we have a piece of chalk?"

On the blackboard he wrote: $w = W$.

"A very clear formula, don't you agree? The little "w" stands for my will, the capital "W" for the will of God. When the two wills run counter to each other, you have the cross. Do you want to get rid of the cross? Then let your will be identified with that of God, who wants you to be saints. Isn't that simple? All you must do is obey!"